D1305236

HOT CHEESE

OVER 50 GOOEY, OOZY, MELTY RECIPES

by **POLINA CHESNAKOVA**

Photographs by Paul Sirisalee

CHRONICLE BOOKS
SAN FRANCISCO

Text copyright © 2020 by Polina Chesnakova.

Photographs copyright © 2020 by Paul Sirisalee.

All rights reserved. No part of this book may be reproduced in any form without written permission from the publisher.

Library of Congress Cataloging-in-Publication Data

Names: Chesnakova, Polina, author. | Sirisalee, Paul, photographer.
Title: Hot cheese : over 50 gooey, oozy, melty recipes /
Polina Chesnakova ; photographs by Paul Sirisalee.
Description: San Francisco : Chronicle Books, [2020] | Includes index. |
Identifiers: LCCN 2019059126 | ISBN 9781452182933 (hardcover)
Subjects: LCSH: Cooking (Cheese) | Cheese. | LCGFT: Cookbooks.
Classification: LCC TX759.5.C48 C525 2020 | DDC 641.6/73—dc23
LC record available at https://lccn.loc.gov/2019059126

Manufactured in China.

Design by Rachel Harrell.

Annie's is a registered trademark of Annie's, Inc. Diamond Crystal Kosher Salt
is a registered trademark of Cargill, Incorporated. Cholula is a registered
trademark of Spicy Liquid, LLC. Google is a registered trademark of Google, LLC.
Guinness is a registered trademark of Diageo Ireland private unlimited company.
Hama Hama Oysters is a registered trademark of Hama Hama Company.
La Choy Chow Mein Noodles is a registered trademark of Conagra Brands.
Ritz Crackers is a registered trademark of Mondelēz International.
Samuel Smith Oatmeal Stout is a registered trademark of Samuel Smith Old
Brewery (Tadcaster). Sterno is a registered trademark of Sterno Products.
Tapatio is a registered trademark of Tapatio Foods, LLC. Velveeta is a registered
trademark of Kraft Foods Group Brands LLC.

10 9 8 7 6 5 4 3 2

Chronicle books and gifts are available at special quantity discounts to corpora-
tions, professional associations, literacy programs, and other organizations. For
details and discount information, please contact our premiums department at
corporatesales@chroniclebooks.com or at 1-800-759-0190.

Chronicle Books LLC
680 Second Street
San Francisco, California 94107
www.chroniclebooks.com

To my family, who introduced me to the allure and magic of hot, melty cheese.

TABLE OF CONTENTS

STARRING MAINS

SUPPORTING SIDES

INTRO

For me, the thrill of hot cheese began decades ago when I was still a child. Born to a Russian-Georgian immigrant family of good cooks and hearty appetites, I was a picky, apathetic eater and a total mystery to them.

I did have, however, one weakness when it came to my family's cuisine: our version of Georgian *khachapuri*. Imagine: golden, flaky pastry that oozed and stretched mozzarella and feta as you pulled a square (or two) off the serving platter. I couldn't help but salivate in anticipation, and as I took my first bite, a small shudder of delight would pass over me as the puff's crispy layers shattered and gave way to gooey, melty cheese. We were convinced (and still are) that no one could resist khachapuri's charms—not even my young, finicky self.

In my years of cooking in specialty cafés and writing about cheese, I've realized something happens when you apply heat to curds: a setting of the stage. A bubbling pot of fondue, a half wheel of Raclette as it blisters and caramelizes under a grill, a baked Camembert waiting to release its molten filling. Hot cheese captivates with its drama and its promise of . . . what? A moment of bliss? A release of inhibitions? Whatever it may be, no one can help but fall under its hypnotizing spell and be captivated by the show.

My desire for this book is that it provides you with that spark of magic. An occasion to light up your burner, gather friends and family around the table, and treat yourselves to hot cheese! You will discover recipes that breathe new life into classics like Smoked Gouda Chicken Cordon Bleu and Tomato and Fennel Soup with Grilled Blue Cheese Croutons, while bringing a whiff of whimsical and international flavors through foods such as Adjaruli Khachapuri, Fried Raclette Sticks with Dill Tartar Sauce, and Korean Bulgogi Cheesesteak with Kimchi. You'll find a perfect mix of special occasions and for those "just because" moments.

The dishes are divided into sections that reflect the way they're consumed: as a finger food, a soup or sandwich for lunchtime, a starring main, a supporting side, or an excuse to gather people together for a celebration. Throughout this book, you will find tips and tricks to strengthen your cheese *and* cooking game, variations to help you play around with flavors, and alternatives for when you can't find that certain fancy wheel or wedge the recipe calls for.

At the heart of hot cheese is an appeal that is both universal and inclusive. So, what are you waiting for? Let's get melting!

BEST CHEESE PRACTICES

To ensure that you find the most success with the recipes in this book, here are a few things to keep in mind:

Recipes were tested with Diamond Crystal kosher salt. If you're cooking with a different variety or brand, go by taste rather than amount.

When measuring flour, spoon the flour into your measuring cup and level it off with the straight edge of a knife or spatula.

I always choose block over pre-shredded cheese (unless I specifically call for it, such as in the enchiladas recipe, page 109). The latter is coated in additives that keep it from clumping in the package, which, as a result, hinders it from reaching its fullest melty cheese potential. The box grater is your best friend when it comes to this book.

Not all cheeses are grated equally—for some recipes, I call for a medium grate and for others, coarse. Because volume can vary significantly depending on the grate size, I include both weight and volume measurements for cheese.

Here are a few measurements to keep in mind:

- Finely grated on a rasp-style grater: 1 oz cheese = ½ slightly packed cup

- Medium grated on a box grater: 1 oz cheese = ⅓ slightly packed cup

- Coarsely grated on a box grater: 1 oz cheese = ¼ slightly packed cup

FINGER FOODS
~~~

CAJUN CHEESY
WAFFLE FRIES

When I was in college in Virginia, there was a dive-y, windowless bar called St. Maarten. The drink specials were wacky (think "Dr. Jones Love Juice") and the interior decor was wanting, to say the least. However, they had these Cajun cheesy waffle fries that kept me, and all of my friends, coming back again and again. St. Maarten has since closed, but in the name of hot cheese, I had to bring these spicy, melty, crispy fries back. For all those Wahoos who loved them as much as I did, these are for you.

Serves 4

One 22 oz [625 g] bag frozen waffle-cut fries

2 tsp Cajun seasoning, plus more for seasoning

6 oz [170 g] sharp Colby Jack cheese, coarsely grated (about 1½ cups)

¼ cup [30 g] crumbled crisped bacon (optional)

Minced fresh chives, for garnish (optional)

Ranch dressing, for serving

1 Preheat the oven to 450°F [230°C]. Line a large baking sheet with aluminum foil.

2 Arrange the frozen fries in a single layer on the prepared baking sheet. Bake for 20 to 25 minutes, flipping them over halfway through, or until the fries are lightly browned and crisped all the way through. Remove from the oven and toss with the Cajun seasoning to evenly coat. Sprinkle with the cheese and bacon, if using. Sprinkle with more Cajun seasoning, if desired. Bake for another 3 to 5 minutes, until the cheese has melted. Top with chives, if desired, and serve immediately with ranch dressing for dipping.

EASY-PEASY
POUTINE

A bed of crispy fries, squeaky cheese curds, and velvety gravy—combine them and you have the iconic, mouthwatering French-Canadian dish called poutine. Of course, the perfect version will have you make the fries from scratch, buy fresh, day-of curds, and whip up a gravy with homemade beef and chicken stock. But sometimes, you just want to cut straight to the hot cheese. And you know what? With the help of a few store-bought items, you can still end up with a version that makes you go gaga. If you are a vegetarian, feel free to substitute the beef and chicken stock for vegetable stock.

Serves 4

1 Bake the french fries according to the package instructions.

2 **Meanwhile, to make the gravy:** In a small bowl, mix the cornstarch and 2 Tbsp of water into a slurry. Set aside.

3 In a medium saucepan, melt the butter over medium-high heat. Add the flour all at once and whisk to make a paste. Cook, stirring constantly, until it turns golden blond, about 2 minutes. Whisk in the shallot, garlic, and thyme and cook for another minute to soften them.

4 Whisking constantly, gradually pour in the beef and chicken stocks, a little bit at a time, in a thin, steady stream. Stir in the ketchup, Worcestershire sauce, vinegar, and cornstarch slurry and bring to a boil. Lower the heat to medium-low and simmer, whisking constantly, until the gravy has thickened, 5 to 6 minutes. Turn the heat to low and season with salt and pepper. Remove the thyme sprig and discard. You want to make sure the gravy is hot when you pour it over the fries and curds, so keep it on low heat while you assemble the poutine. Stored in an airtight container, the gravy will last for up to 2 days in the refrigerator—just bring it to a boil over high heat before continuing.

5 Transfer the fries to individual dishes or one large platter. Top with the cheese curds. Ladle the hot gravy over the fries and cheese curds, making sure you coat everything. Sprinkle with freshly ground black pepper and chives and let it sit for 1 to 2 minutes to let the curds melt a bit before serving.

One 28 or 32 oz [795 or 910 g] bag frozen french fries

—

GRAVY

2 Tbsp cornstarch

4 Tbsp [55 g] unsalted butter

¼ cup [35 g] all-purpose flour

1 small shallot, minced (2½ to 3 Tbsp)

1 garlic clove, minced

1 large fresh thyme sprig

3 cups [720 ml] store-bought or homemade beef stock or broth

1 cup [240 ml] store-bought or homemade chicken stock or broth (or more beef stock)

2 Tbsp ketchup

2 tsp Worcestershire sauce

1 tsp apple cider vinegar or rice vinegar

Kosher salt

Freshly ground black pepper

—

7 to 10 oz [200 to 280 g] fresh cheese curds (or low-moisture mozzarella cheese, cut into bite-size cubes), at room temperature (1½ to 2 cups)

Minced fresh chives, for garnish

CACIO E PEPE

GOUGÈRES

These cheese puffs, also known as French gougères, receive the literal *cacio e pepe* ("cheese and pepper") treatment in this fun twist on the traditional Roman pasta dish. Loaded with salty pecorino romano—an Italian aged sheep's milk cheese—and freshly cracked black pepper in each bite, they are as hard to resist as they are easy to make. These are best eaten while still warm.

Makes about 3 dozen cheese puffs

1 Preheat the oven to 425°F [220°C]. Line two baking sheets with parchment paper.

2 In a small, heavy-bottomed saucepan, combine ½ cup [120 ml] of water, the milk, butter, and salt and warm over medium heat until the butter melts.

3 Once the butter has melted, add the flour all at once and begin to stir vigorously with a wooden spoon until the mixture pulls away from the sides of the pan into a smooth ball. Continue to cook, stirring constantly, for another 2 to 3 minutes, or until the dough smells nutty and glistens, and a thin film develops on the bottom of the saucepan.

4 Transfer the dough to the bowl of a stand mixer fitted with the paddle attachment. Beat on low speed until all the steam escapes and the dough feels slightly warm to the touch, 1 to 2 minutes.

5 Increase the speed to medium-high and add 4 of the eggs one at a time. Allow for each egg to fully incorporate, scraping the sides of the work bowl if needed, before you add the next one. The mixture might turn lumpy at first, but then it will come together and turn smooth and glossy. Stir in the cheese and black pepper.

6 Pipe the dough into 1 Tbsp mounds on the prepared baking sheets, allowing 1 in [2.5 cm] of space between each mound. Alternatively, you can use a spoon to scoop 1 rounded Tbsp of dough and use another spoon to push it onto the baking sheet. The gougères can be frozen for up to 2 months. Before baking straight from the freezer, be sure to brush with the egg wash and garnish, and allow a few extra minutes in the oven.

7 In a small bowl, lightly beat the remaining egg with the heavy cream. Brush each mound with the egg wash. Sprinkle generously with more grated cheese and a dusting of black pepper.

8 Transfer to the oven and bake for 10 minutes, allowing the gougères to puff up and rise. Without opening the oven, decrease the heat to 375°F [190°C] and bake for 15 to 20 minutes more, until the gougères are golden and firm. About 5 minutes before they're done, poke a hole into each gougère with a sharp knife to release steam and return to the oven to finish baking. Serve while still warm or at room temperature.

½ cup [120 ml] whole milk

6 Tbsp [85 g] unsalted butter, cubed

1½ tsp kosher salt

1 cup [140 g] all-purpose flour

5 eggs

4½ oz [130 g] pecorino romano cheese, medium grated (about 1⅓ cups), plus more for garnish

1 tsp freshly ground black pepper, plus more for garnish

1 Tbsp heavy cream, whole milk, or water

FRIED

RACLETTE STICKS

WITH DILL TARTAR SAUCE

Forget mozzarella. What you really want in this nostalgic appetizer is the salty, funky, and supreme melter Raclette. Onion powder and granulated garlic in the breading echo the funkiness of the Swiss cow's milk cheese, while the bright acidity of the dill pickle tartar sauce cuts through the fat. Double coating ensures not only that the outside gets nice and crispy, but also that the inside has enough time to melt without oozing out. Don't skip on the panko for regular bread crumbs—it adds that extra crunch factor!

Makes 24 cheese sticks

1 Line a baking sheet with parchment paper.

2 **To make the Raclette sticks:** Put the bread crumbs, flour, and eggs in separate shallow bowls. In the bowl with the bread crumbs, add the onion powder, granulated garlic, and black pepper and mix to combine.

3 Working with one cheese stick at a time, dredge it in the flour to fully coat and shake off the excess. Dip it in the eggs, then coat it in the bread crumbs. Repeat the process again for a second coating. Place on the prepared baking sheet, and repeat with the rest of the cheese sticks. Freeze the sticks for at least 2 hours and up to 3 days.

RACLETTE STICKS

2 cups [120 g] panko bread crumbs

¾ cup [105 g] all-purpose flour

4 eggs, lightly beaten

1½ tsp onion powder

1½ tsp granulated garlic, or ¾ tsp garlic powder

1½ tsp freshly ground black pepper

1 lb [455 g] Raclette cheese, rind removed, cut into 3 by ½ in [7.5 cm by 12 mm] sticks

About 6 cups [1.4 L] vegetable or canola oil

—

TARTAR SAUCE

½ cup [120 g] mayonnaise

¼ cup finely chopped dill pickles

2 Tbsp dill pickle juice

1 Tbsp capers

2 tsp finely chopped fresh dill

4 **To make the tartar sauce:** Just before you fry the Raclette sticks, place all the ingredients for the tartar sauce in a food processor and pulse a few times until fully mixed, but not puréed. Transfer to a dipping bowl and set aside.

5 Preheat the oven to 200°F [95°C]. Line another baking sheet with parchment paper and place it inside the oven while it heats. Line a large plate with a paper towel and have it ready nearby.

6 Meanwhile, fit a large pot with a deep-fry thermometer and pour in the oil to a depth of 2 in [5 cm]. Heat over medium heat until the temperature reaches 350°F [180°C]. Working in batches of 3 sticks at a time, fry the cheese sticks on one side for 1 minute. Flip over and fry for another minute, until golden brown and crispy all around. Transfer to the paper towel–lined plate to soak up any excess oil and then transfer the sticks to the oven to keep warm while you finish frying the rest. Serve with the tartar sauce.

JALAPEÑO POPPER
PIGS IN A BLANKET

Smoky franks and flaky, buttery pastry meet creamy cheese and hot jalapeños—do you love me yet? Although the heat of the oven tempers the peppers' heat, this mash-up of America's beloved finger foods still packs a kick. Nonetheless, I find them painfully addictive, so consider yourself warned. They're best washed down with a cold pint of beer.

Makes 24 pigs

1 Preheat the oven to 375°F [190°C]. Line a large baking sheet with parchment paper.

2 In a small bowl, combine the cream cheese, Cheddar, and lime juice. Set aside.

3 Cut each jalapeño half in half again lengthwise, and then again cross-wise. You should get 24 pieces.

4 Spoon about 1 tsp of the cheese mixture onto each jalapeño piece and then top with a frank, pressing down to adhere the components together. Set aside.

5 Open and roll out the crescent roll dough and tear it into triangles along the perforated lines. Evenly cut each triangle lengthwise into three narrower triangles. Place a jalapeño-frank on the wider end of one of these triangles and roll it up. Transfer it to the prepared baking sheet, point-side down. Repeat with the remaining franks, leaving 1½ to 2 in [4 to 5 cm] of space between each piece.

6 Pop in the refrigerator for 5 to 10 minutes to firm up the dough (or cover with plastic wrap and store in the refrigerator for up to 2 hours before continuing).

7 Meanwhile, in a small bowl, combine the egg and cream.

8 Remove the tray from the refrigerator and brush each pastry with the egg wash. Sprinkle with flaky sea salt. Bake until the pastry is golden brown, 12 to 15 minutes. Let sit for a few minutes before transferring to a serving platter. Serve while still warm.

4 oz [115 g] cream cheese, at room temperature

4 oz [115 g] sharp Cheddar cheese, coarsely grated (about 1 cup)

1 Tbsp fresh lime juice

3 large jalapeño peppers, stemmed, halved, and seeded

24 beef cocktail franks

One 8 oz [225 g] can refrigerated crescent roll dough

1 egg, lightly beaten

1 Tbsp heavy cream, milk, or water

Flaky sea salt

To make Everything Bagel Pigs in a Blanket: Omit the jalapeño, substitute lemon juice for lime juice, and spread 1 tsp of cream cheese mixture onto each small crescent roll triangle and roll up. Sprinkle each egg-washed pastry with everything bagel seasoning instead of flaky sea salt and bake as directed.

SPINACH, FETA, AND
MOZZARELLA
TURNOVERS

Love spanakopita but don't want to deal with finicky phyllo dough? Then these fun puff pastries are for you. It doesn't hurt that you probably have many of these ingredients already on hand, too. They're baked to golden, flaky perfection and are a welcome addition to any holiday meal or game day spread, or even as an afternoon snack.

Makes 18 small turnovers

1 In a large skillet, heat the olive oil over medium heat. Add the yellow onion and a pinch of salt and cook, stirring frequently, for 7 to 8 minutes, or until the onion begins to brown. Add the garlic and red pepper flakes and cook for 1 minute more. Add the spinach and cook until thawed and warmed through, 2 to 3 minutes. Remove from the heat and transfer to a bowl.

2 Once the spinach mixture has cooled, stir in the mozzarella, feta, green onions, dill, and lemon zest until fully mixed. Season with salt and red pepper flakes, as desired. You can cover and refrigerate the filling for up to 5 days before assembling the pastries.

3 Line two baking sheets with parchment paper. In a small bowl,

combine the egg and heavy cream and set aside.

4 On a lightly floured surface, roll 1 puff pastry sheet into a 9 in [23 cm] square. Cut into nine 3 by 3 in [7.5 by 7.5 cm] squares and place 2 Tbsp of filling into the center of each square. Lightly brush the edges of the pastries with the egg wash. Fold each square in half to form a triangle and seal the edges by pinching them together. Transfer the pastries to the prepared baking sheet and refrigerate while you repeat the process with the remaining puff pastry sheet. Refrigerate the assembled pastries to firm up the dough, 15 to 20 minutes. They can keep, covered and refrigerated, for a few hours.

5 When ready to bake, position racks in the lower and upper thirds of the oven. Preheat the oven to 400°F [200°C].

6 Remove pastries from the refrigerator and use a fork to crimp the edges, making sure they are well sealed. Brush each pastry with egg wash and sprinkle with black and white sesame seeds and flaky sea salt. Cut small vents into the pastries. Assembled unbaked pastries can be stored in the freezer for up to

1 Tbsp extra-virgin olive oil

1 small yellow onion, finely chopped

Kosher salt

1 garlic clove, cut into thin slices

¼ tsp red pepper flakes, plus more as desired

1 cup [100 g] frozen spinach (or cooked spinach, well squeezed and finely chopped)

4 oz [115 g] low-moisture part-skim mozzarella cheese, coarsely grated (about 1 cup)

2 oz [60 g] crumbled feta (about ½ cup)

2 green onions, green top removed, cut into thin slices

1 to 2 Tbsp finely chopped fresh dill

1 tsp lemon zest

1 egg, lightly beaten

1 Tbsp heavy cream, whole milk, or water

2 frozen puff pastry sheets, thawed but chilled

Black sesame seeds, for garnish

White sesame seeds, for garnish

Flaky sea salt, for garnish

3 months—just add a few extra minutes to the baking time. Bake the pastries, rotating the sheets from top to bottom and back to front halfway through, until they are puffed up, golden brown, and firm to the touch, 15 to 20 minutes. Serve while still hot.

MINI

LEMON-BASIL

ARANCINI

These little bites are a labor of love, but I can't stress how worth it they are. The Sicilian recipe begins with risotto, which I've chosen to brighten with lemon and aromatic basil. The rice is then chilled overnight, formed into little balls, stuffed with mozzarella, and lastly breaded. Once deep-fried, the outside becomes a golden crisp shell that, when shattered, reveals creamy risotto and a molten center of cheese. Your guests will sing your praises, and feel free to give yourself a pat on the back, too.

I've made them mini to make serving a large crowd easier (plus they're so cute!), but if you want to minimize work, I've included a regular-size variation that will work as a great appetizer for 4 to 6.

Makes about 40 mini or 14 regular arancini

1 In a medium saucepan, bring the stock to a simmer. Keep warm on low heat.

2 In a large pot, heat the butter and olive oil over medium heat. Add the onion and a big pinch of salt and cook until the onion begins to soften, about 5 minutes. Add the garlic and cook for 1 minute more.

3 Add the rice and another big pinch of salt and stir to fully coat it with the butter and oil. Cook for another 2 to 3 minutes (the edges will begin to look translucent). Pour in the wine and cook, stirring frequently, until the liquid is almost fully evaporated, another 2 minutes.

4 Ladle in ½ cup [120 ml] of the warmed broth and cook, stirring constantly, until the broth is absorbed, another 2 to 3 minutes. Continue in this way, adding ½ cup [120 ml] at a time and stirring constantly, until the rice is cooked but still slightly firm to the teeth, 20 to 25 minutes. Stir in the Parmesan, lemon juice, zest, and basil. Season with salt and pepper. Let cool completely before refrigerating, covered, overnight. The rice

-cont.

4 cups [960 ml] store-bought or homemade chicken or vegetable stock or broth

2 Tbsp butter

1 Tbsp extra-virgin olive oil

1 medium onion, finely chopped

Kosher salt

2 garlic cloves, cut into thin slices

1 cup [215 g] Arborio or carnaroli rice

½ cup [120 ml] dry white wine

2 oz [55 g] fresh Parmesan cheese, medium grated (about ⅔ cup)

1 Tbsp fresh lemon juice

1½ tsp lemon zest (from about ½ lemon)

¼ cup [10 g] finely chopped fresh basil

Freshly ground black pepper

40 perline (pearl-size) mozzarella cheese balls, drained

1¼ cups [170 g] all-purpose flour

1 egg, lightly beaten

2 cups [120 g] panko bread crumbs

About 6 cups [1.4 L] vegetable oil, for frying

can be made up to 5 days in advance, stored in an airtight container, and refrigerated.

5 Line a baking sheet with parchment paper.

6 Roll 1 Tbsp risotto in your hand and make an indent in the middle. Fill it with 1 perline mozzarella ball and plug up the hole with a bit more rice—it should be about 1¼ in [3 cm] in diameter, but it's OK if it's not exact. Transfer to the baking sheet. Repeat the process until all the risotto is used up. The risotto balls can be wrapped in plastic and refrigerated for up to 3 days.

7 In a small mixing bowl, mix the flour, egg, and enough water (about ¾ cup [180 ml]) to make a thick batter. Season with ¾ tsp of salt and some pepper.

8 Pulse the panko in a food processor or put in a large zip-top bag and bang it with a rolling pin until finely ground. Place the panko in a shallow bowl and season with salt and pepper.

9 Lightly dip the sides of a rice ball (rather than fully sub-merging it) in the thick batter until evenly coated. Then transfer to the panko and roll it to fully coat. Transfer to the baking sheet and repeat with the remaining rice balls.

10 Preheat the oven to 200°F [95°C]. Line a baking sheet with parchment paper and place it in the oven while it heats. Line a large plate with paper towels and have it ready nearby.

11 Meanwhile, fit a medium heavy-bottomed pot with a deep-fry thermometer and pour in oil to a depth of 2 in [5 cm]. Heat over medium heat until the temperature reaches 350°F [180°C].

12 Working in batches of 3 or 4 risotto balls, use a slotted spoon or spider to carefully lower them into the oil. Cook until they turn a deep golden brown, about 2 minutes. Transfer to the paper towel–lined plate to drain. You can either wait for them to cool slightly before serving immediately or, if you'd like to serve them all at once, put the arancini in the oven while you continue to fry the rest of the uncooked balls.

13 Arancini can be cooled completely and kept at room temperature for a few hours, refrigerated for up to 2 days, or frozen for up to 2 months before being reheated in a 350°F [180°C] oven until they are warmed through and the cheese is melty.

To make regular-size arancini: Scoop about 2 Tbsp cooked risotto and form into a ball. Fill with 3 perline mozzarella balls (or 1 ciliegine, or "cherry-size," mozzarella ball) and plug up the hole with a bit more rice. They should be about 2 in [5 cm] in diameter, and you should get about 14 balls. Follow the rest of the instructions for the mini arancini, but fry for 1 minute longer for a total of about 3 minutes.

FROMAGE

FORT TOASTS

It's not hard to imagine that during the course of writing this book, there was never a moment when my fridge was not packed with various wheels and wedges. When I found myself with too many random nubs, I'd turn to *fromage fort*—a strong cheese spread made from those bits and pieces, along with garlic and white wine. Serve it cold or, even better, broiled until melty and browned over toast.

Use whatever cheese you need to use up, but keep in mind that a blue can easily overpower if there's too much. Soft varieties like Taleggio, triple-crèmes, and chèvres will help make the paste more spreadable, but if you have mostly harder wedges, add a bit of cream cheese to smooth it out. You never know what flavor profile you'll get—and that's half the fun.

This recipe was adapted from Jacques Pépin by way of my dear friend Molly Reeder's mother.

Serves 6 to 8 as an appetizer

1 In the bowl of a food processor, add the cheese pieces, 1 oz [30 g] of cream cheese (if using), the wine, garlic, and 4 or 5 grinds of black pepper. Process, scraping down the sides as needed, until the mixture is smooth and creamy. If it's not homogenized enough, add the remaining 1 oz [30 g] cream cheese and purée until smooth. Add the chives (if using) and pulse until incorporated. The paste usually doesn't need salt but taste and season if needed. The fromage fort can be stored in an airtight container and refrigerated for up to 1 week (but beware, it will get stronger) or frozen for up to 2 months.

2 Turn the broiler on high. Line a baking sheet with aluminum foil.

3 Place the bread slices on the baking sheet and spread each slice with the fromage fort. Broil until the cheese is melty, begins to brown, and is wonderfully aromatic, anywhere from 1 to 4 minutes depending on the strength of your broiler. Sprinkle with more chives, if desired, and black pepper. Serve immediately.

8 oz [230 g] assorted cheeses, hard rinds removed, cut into bite-size pieces

1 to 2 oz [30 to 55 g] cream cheese, at room temperature (optional)

¼ cup [60 ml] dry white wine or hard cider

1 garlic clove, minced

Freshly ground black pepper

1 Tbsp minced chives or fresh flat-leaf parsley, plus more for garnish (optional)

Kosher salt

Baguette, cut into ½ in [12 mm] diagonal slices

SPECK-WRAPPED

DATES STUFFED

WITH GORGONZOLA PICCANTE

20 to 24 soft, plump Medjool dates

4 oz [110 g] Gorgonzola piccante

20 to 24 thin slices speck

These aren't your average bacon-wrapped dates. Plump Medjool dates are stuffed with *Gorgonzola piccante*, a pungent and spicy Italian cow's milk blue that holds its own amid the strong flavors, before being wrapped with speck—a smoked prosciutto rubbed with spices like juniper and bay leaves from the northern part of Italy. When broiled, the salty, smoky pork turns crisp, the sweet-lush fruit blisters, and the soft cheese begins to wonderfully ooze. They'll disappear from the table before you know it.

If you can't find speck, regular or even spicy prosciutto makes a delicious substitute; and if you can't find Gorgonzola piccante, look for another blue with a similar kick, such as French Roquefort or Spanish Valdeón. Funky Taleggio or creamy chèvre would also work well here.

Makes 20 to 24 dates

1 Position a rack in the upper third of the oven and turn the broiler on high. Line a baking sheet with parchment paper.

2 Use a paring knife to cut a lengthwise slit into one side of each date. Carefully remove the pits, making sure you don't break the date in half.

3 Stuff each date with chunks of Gorgonzola and wrap in speck. Transfer to the prepared baking sheet seam-side down.

4 Broil for 4 to 5 minutes, or until the speck has crisped up and the cheese begins to bubble and ooze. The dates will be extremely hot to handle and eat, so allow them to cool for a few minutes before serving.

STUFFED
MUSH-ROOMS
WITH MANCHEGO AND CHÈVRE

These stuffed mushrooms are inspired by the flavors of Spain and are a nod to the popular tapas dish *champiñones al ajillo*. Bright fresh chèvre serves as the creamy base to which rich, zesty Manchego, sweet roasted piquillo peppers, parsley, and lemon are added. A crispy bread crumb topping rounds out the bite—and puts this simple party snack over the top.

Look for a Manchego that's aged for ideally 3 to 6 months—it will melt better here—versus 12 months. Roasted piquillo peppers are usually sold in jars, but if you can't find them, regular roasted red peppers will make a good substitution.

Makes about 24 stuffed mushrooms

1 Preheat the oven to 400°F [200°C]. Butter or oil a large baking sheet.

2 Remove the stem from each mushroom. Set the caps aside and finely chop the stems. Heat 1 Tbsp of the olive oil in a skillet over medium heat. Add the chopped stems and cook, stirring occasionally, until they begin to brown, about 5 minutes. Add the garlic and cook for 1 minute more. Season with salt and transfer to a medium bowl.

3 Let cool slightly and then add the chèvre, 3 oz (1 cup [85 g]) of the Manchego, the peppers, parsley, and lemon zest. Mix to combine. Season with salt. The filling can be stored in an airtight container and refrigerated for up to 2 days in advance.

4 Fill the cavity of each mushroom with the cheese mixture, creating a small mound. There might be some filling left over. Transfer the mushroom caps to the prepared baking sheet. The stuffed mushrooms can be made up to 2 days in advance, covered, and refrigerated.

5 In a small bowl, drizzle the remaining 1 Tbsp of oil over the bread crumbs. Stir in the remaining 2 Tbsp of Manchego and use your fingers to combine the mixture until the bread crumbs are fully saturated with oil. Season with salt and pepper. Press the filled side of each mushroom into the bread crumbs to coat.

6 Bake the mushrooms on the prepared baking sheet until the tops are golden brown, 15 to 20 minutes. Garnish with parsley and serve immediately.

1 lb [455 g] large cremini mushrooms (about 24)

2 Tbsp extra-virgin olive oil

2 garlic cloves, minced

Kosher salt

4 oz [85 g] fresh chèvre, at room temperature

3 oz plus 2 Tbsp [90 g] 3- or 6-month Manchego cheese, medium grated (about 1 cup plus 2 Tbsp)

3 roasted piquillo peppers, rinsed, drained, and finely chopped (about ¼ cup)

2 Tbsp finely chopped fresh flat-leaf parsley, plus more for garnish

1½ tsp fresh lemon zest

¼ cup [15 g] panko bread crumbs

Freshly ground black pepper

LUNCH-
TIME

~~~~~

BACON, BRIE, AND PEPPER JELLY
PANINI
WITH ARUGULA

While I was working at a gourmet market, the most popular sandwiches sold were a simple but delicious combination of cheese, meat, and a sweet spread. Taking a note from the market's book, enter this sweet-and-savory panini featuring buttery Brie contrasted with smoky, crispy bacon and a punch of sweet and spicy red pepper jelly.

Makes 4 sandwiches

1 Heat a panini press according to the manufacturer's instructions (if using).

2 In a small bowl, combine the mayonnaise and mustard. Set aside.

3 Butter one side of each slice of bread or the outside of the roll halves. Flip over and spread a thin layer of pepper jelly on half of the bread slices. Place 3 slices of Brie on top and then 3 slices of bacon. Evenly spread the remaining bread slices with the mayo-mustard and cover the assembled sandwiches, mayo-side down.

4 Cook on a panini press until the bread is toasted and browned and the cheese is melted, 3 to 4 minutes. Alternatively, heat a ridged grill pan or cast-iron skillet over medium-low heat. Place the sandwiches, working in batches if needed, in the pan and weight down with another heavy skillet. Cook until the bottoms are golden brown and crispy, 3 to 4 minutes. Flip, weight down with the skillet, and cook on medium-low heat for another 3 to 4 minutes, or until the bread is browned and the cheese is melted.

5 Transfer the sandwiches to a cutting board. Open and distribute the arugula evenly between them. Reassemble the sandwiches and cut in half before serving hot.

3 Tbsp mayonnaise

3 Tbsp whole grain mustard

Butter, for spreading

8 sourdough bread slices, or 4 rolls ciabatta bread halved crosswise

¼ to ⅓ cup [75 to 100 g] good-quality mild or hot red pepper jelly

8 oz [230 g] Brie wheel, cut into ¼ in [6 mm] thick slices

12 crisped slices applewood-smoked bacon

1 cup [20 g] baby arugula

CROQUE
MONSIEUR

When I think (OK, dream) of French bistro food, my mind immediately wanders to a croque monsieur—a glorified ham and Gruyère grilled cheese with béchamel smeared on the inside as well as spooned over the top. If that's not enough, a final layer of Gruyère is sprinkled over the white creamy sauce and then it all goes under a broiler to melt, sizzle, and brown. Topped with a sunny-side up egg, it becomes a croque madame and the cue for a nap.

Makes 2 sandwiches

1 In a medium saucepan, melt the butter over medium heat. Add the flour all at once and quickly whisk into a paste. Continue to cook, whisking constantly, until it smells biscuity, 1 to 1½ minutes—don't let it brown. Gradually pour in the milk, a bit at a time, whisking constantly and thoroughly after each addition. Make sure you get into all corners of the pan to ensure a smooth, lump-free texture. The paste will initially become thick and then turn very thin once all the milk has been added. Bring to a boil. Continue to cook, stirring constantly, until the sauce is thick enough to coat

the back of a spoon, 4 to 5 minutes. Season with salt and nutmeg and remove from the heat. The béchamel can be made ahead and stored, covering the top with plastic wrap to prevent a skin from forming, in an airtight container in the refrigerator for up to 2 days.

2 Butter the bread slices on one side, making sure you go all the way to the edges. Flip over and spread 2 of the slices generously with béchamel, reserving some for the topping. If using, lightly spread the other 2 slices with mustard. Divide the ham between the two béchamel-covered slices and sprinkle with ½ cup (2 oz [55 g]) cheese each. Top with the remaining slices, mustard-side down.

3 Position a rack in the upper third of the oven and turn the broiler on high. Heat a large ovenproof skillet over medium-low heat. Place the sandwiches cheese-side down and cook until the bottoms are browned and crispy, 3 to 4 minutes. Flip and cook until the other side is also browned, another 3 to 4 minutes. If your skillet is not big enough to hold both sandwiches, work with

one at a time and transfer to a small baking sheet. Generously slather the tops with béchamel (you will have sauce left over) and sprinkle with the remaining ¼ cup (1 oz [30 g]) cheese. Broil until the cheese topping is bubbly and lightly browned, 2 to 5 minutes. Let sit for a few minutes before cutting in half and serving.

1½ Tbsp unsalted butter, plus more, at room temperature, for spreading

1½ Tbsp all-purpose flour

1 cup [240 ml] whole milk, hot

Kosher salt

Pinch of freshly grated nutmeg

4 slices country-style or sourdough bread

Dijon mustard (optional)

4 slices French or Black Forest ham

5 oz [140 g] Gruyère, Comté, or Emmental cheese, coarsely grated (about 1¼ cups)

GREENWOOD'S

MEATBALL SUB

The meatballs in tomato sauce from Greenwood Gourmet Grocery in Crozet, Virginia, is a menu staple for a reason: Tender, juicy meatballs swim in a fennel, oregano, and thyme sauce reminiscent of your favorite store-bought marinara, but with much more depth and body. I've adapted their recipe for one of my favorite sandwiches: a meatball sub. Just nestle them into a hoagie roll smeared with pesto, top with melty, gooey cheese, and you've got yourself a winning combo.

If you're in a pinch, though, it will do just fine to cook the meatballs in store-bought marinara.

Makes 16 meatballs for 4 sandwiches

1 In a medium skillet, heat the butter over medium heat and add the onion and a pinch of salt. Cook until the onion begins to soften and turn translucent, about 5 minutes. Add the oregano, thyme, crushed fennel seeds, and red pepper flakes and cook for 1 minute more. Remove from the heat, scrape into a large bowl, and let cool completely.

2 To the cooled onion mixture, add the ground beef, Parmesan cheese, egg, bread crumbs, milk, garlic, and 1½ tsp salt. Using your hands, gently and quickly mix the meat by pinching it through your fingers, rather than kneading it, until everything comes together and is just combined (do not overmix). The meat can be mixed and refrigerated up to 1 day in advance.

3 Wet your hands, lightly form and roll the meat (don't pack it too tight) into 1½ in [4 cm] balls, and put them on a large plate. You should have about 16 meatballs.

4 In a large Dutch oven, pot, or saucepan with deep sides, bring the tomato sauce to a simmer over medium-low heat. Gently nestle the meatballs, one by one, into the sauce and cover. Turn the heat to low and cook, gently rotating them in the sauce halfway through, for about 30 minutes or until cooked through. You can remove one and cut it in half to make sure.

2 Tbsp unsalted butter

½ medium yellow onion, finely chopped

Kosher salt

1½ tsp dried oregano

1½ tsp dried thyme

1 tsp fennel seeds, crushed

¾ tsp red pepper flakes

1 lb [455 g] 80 or 85% lean ground beef

2 oz [55 g] coarsely grated fresh Parmesan or grana Padano cheese (about ½ cup)

1 egg, lightly beaten

½ cup [30 g] panko bread crumbs

⅓ cup [80 ml] whole milk

1 garlic clove, minced

Tomato Sauce (recipe follows), or one 24 oz [680 g] jar store-bought marinara sauce

4 hoagie rolls or 5 to 6 in [12 to 15 cm] pieces French baguette

½ cup [125 g] pesto

8 slices provolone cheese

5 Position a rack in the middle of the oven and turn the broiler on high.

6 Butterfly the rolls lengthwise. Spread the inside of the rolls or all of the baguette pieces with pesto and nestle 4 meatballs inside with the sauce. Top with 2 slices of provolone cheese. Transfer to a baking sheet and broil until the cheese melts, 2 to 5 minutes. Serve immediately.

TOMATO SAUCE

Makes about 3 cups [710 ml]

1 In a large Dutch oven, pot, or saucepan with deep sides, heat the oil over medium heat. Add the onion and a pinch of salt and cook until the onion begins to soften, about 5 minutes. Add the garlic, oregano, basil, sugar, thyme, and red pepper flakes, and cook for 1 minute. Deglaze the pan with the red wine, stirring to scrape up the browned bits from the bottom of the pot, and cook for 1 minute more.

2 Add the crushed tomatoes, bay leaf, and another pinch of salt and bring to a simmer. Continue to cook over medium heat, stirring occasionally, for about 20 minutes, or until the sauce thickens. Season with salt. Remove the bay leaf and leave the sauce as it is or purée it with an immersion blender to make it smooth. The sauce can be cooled, covered, and kept in the refrigerator for up to 2 days. Rewarm before continuing with the recipe.

2 Tbsp olive oil

½ medium yellow onion, finely chopped

Kosher salt

2 garlic cloves, minced

¾ tsp dried oregano, or 1½ Tbsp finely chopped fresh oregano

¾ tsp dried basil, or 1½ Tbsp finely chopped fresh basil

½ tsp granulated sugar

Heaping ¼ tsp dried thyme

Pinch of red pepper flakes

2 Tbsp red wine

One 28 oz [795 g] can crushed tomatoes

1 fresh or dried bay leaf

KOREAN BULGOGI

CHEESE-STEAK

WITH KIMCHI

Fusion cuisine has a complicated reputation in the food world, but in this instance, it really, *really* works. Thinly sliced steak marinated in spicy and sweet Korean bulgogi sauce is given the Philly treatment with a hot sear, browned onions and peppers, and a blanket of melted pepper Jack. Throw kimchi into the mix for a bright and crunchy foil, and you may never want a regular ol' cheesesteak again. To save time, you can usually find shaved steak at most grocery stores or well-stocked Asian markets. Alternatively, you can call ahead to ask your butcher to thinly slice it for you. Take note that the meat needs to be marinated overnight to tenderize and infuse it with flavor.

Makes 4 sandwiches

1 Wrap the steak in plastic wrap, transfer to a baking sheet, and put in the freezer for 1 to 2 hours, depending on your cut—you want to firm it enough so that the knife goes smoothly through it when you slice. Meanwhile, make the bulgogi marinade (recipe follows).

2 When the meat is partially frozen, take it out and slice it as thinly as you can, working against the grain (if the meat is too soft, put it back in the freezer). Roughly chop the slices if they're long. Transfer the meat to a medium bowl and pour the bulgogi marinade over it. Gently massage the marinade into the beef. Refrigerate the meat for at least 4 hours and ideally overnight.

3 In a large cast-iron skillet, heat 1 Tbsp of the oil over medium-high heat. Add the onion, bell pepper, and a pinch of salt and cook, stirring occasionally, until softened and starting to brown, 8 to 10 minutes. Transfer to a plate or bowl and set aside.

4 In the now-empty skillet, heat the remaining 1 Tbsp of oil over medium-high heat. Working in

-cont.

1½ lb [680 g] well-marbled, boneless rib-eye, skirt, or sirloin steak

Bulgogi Marinade (recipe follows)

2 Tbsp vegetable or grapeseed oil, plus more as needed

1 medium yellow onion, cut into ¼ in [6 mm] slices

1 red bell pepper, cored, seeded, and cut into ¼ in [6 mm] slices

Kosher salt

1 cup [100 g] kimchi, drained, plus 1½ tsp kimchi juice reserved from jar

¼ cup [60 g] mayonnaise

4 long crusty rolls

8 slices pepper Jack cheese

Thinly sliced green onions, for garnish

Fresh cilantro leaves, for garnish

Sesame seeds, for garnish

batches, add the steak to the pan in a single layer and cook without moving for 1 minute. Toss the meat and continue to cook, stirring occasionally, until the meat is cooked through, another 1 to 2 minutes. Season with salt if necessary. Transfer to the plate with the onions and peppers and repeat the process with the remaining meat, adding more oil and salt as needed. When the last batch of meat is done cooking, remove from the heat and add the onions, peppers, and cooked meat back into the skillet and mix to combine.

5 Position a rack in the middle of the oven and turn the broiler on high.

6 In a small bowl, combine the kimchi juice and mayonnaise.

7 Butterfly the rolls lengthwise. Smear the inside of each roll with the mayonnaise mixture. Divide the meat among the rolls, followed by the kimchi. Top each sandwich with 2 slices of pepper Jack (it may seem like a lot of cheese, but it's a cheese-steak after all!). Transfer to a baking sheet and broil until the cheese melts, 2 to 5 minutes. Remove from the oven and top with the green onions, cilantro, and a sprinkle of sesame seeds. Serve immediately.

BULGOGI MARINADE

~~~

Makes about ½ cup [120 g]

1 Put all the ingredients into the bowl of a small food processor and process until smooth. The marinade can be made 1 day in advance.

————

½ Asian or Bosc pear, peeled and roughly chopped

¼ cup [60 ml] soy sauce or tamari

2 Tbsp light brown sugar

1 Tbsp toasted sesame oil

1 Tbsp gochujang hot sauce or Sriracha

4 garlic cloves, roughly chopped

1½ in [4 cm] piece ginger, peeled and roughly chopped

MY KIND OF
GRILLED CHEESE

I love caramelized onions in my grilled cheese, but I don't always have the patience to cook them. Thankfully, leeks turn buttery and melty in half the time. A splash of vinegar adds brightness to the rich filling, while mixing the cheese and leeks together ensures perfectly balanced bites. Mayonnaise (not butter) on the outside produces an even, nicely browned and slightly tangy crust. With so few components involved, seek out the best-quality ingredients that you can find.

Feel free to experiment and find your own ultimate grilled cheese components. Think bacon, *soppressata* or prosciutto, kimchi, savory chutney, pepper jelly, or pickled jalapeño. In lieu of leeks, try juicy, ripe tomato slices. Swap out Cheddar for Gruyère, Comté, fontina, Havarti, Taleggio, Gouda, or Brie. The sky's the limit!

Makes 2 sandwiches

1 In a large nonstick skillet, melt the butter over medium-low heat. Add the leek, garlic, and a big pinch of salt and cook until the leeks soften and begin to brown, about 10 minutes. Stir in the vinegar and cook for another 1 to 2 minutes, or until the liquid evaporates and the leeks begin to dry out again. Remove from the heat and transfer to a medium bowl. Season with salt and let cool. Wipe out the skillet or wash it if necessary.

2 Add the cheeses to the slightly cooled leeks and mix to combine. Spread one side of each bread slice all the way to the edges with a thin layer of mayonnaise. Flip over and divide the cheese-leek mixture evenly between 2 of the slices. Sprinkle with paprika (if using). Top with the remaining slices of bread (mayo-side up) and press down.

3 Heat the skillet over medium-low heat. Add the sandwiches and cook until the bottoms are crispy and brown, 3 to 4 minutes. Flip over and cook, pressing down again, until the cheese is melty and the bottoms are golden brown, another 3 to 4 minutes. Serve immediately.

1 Tbsp unsalted butter

1 large leek, washed thoroughly (see Note, page 118), dark green top removed, cut into thin slices

2 garlic cloves, cut into thin slices

Kosher salt

2 tsp dry white wine vinegar or sherry vinegar

4 oz [115 g] good-quality sharp Cheddar cheese, coarsely grated (1 cup)

½ oz [15 g] fresh Parmesan cheese, finely grated (¼ cup)

4 thick slices sourdough or hearty white bread

Mayonnaise, for spreading

Paprika (optional)

HERBED MUSHROOM AND GOUDA
TARTINE

As someone who can eat a whole pan's worth of mushrooms (and cheese), this tartine is my ideal. Hearty bread is heaped with sautéed garlicky and herbed mushrooms and then blessed with a generous mound of buttery young Gouda. While baking, the Gouda melts down and forms pools on the side of the toast that, with the help of the broiler, turn into crunchy cheese crisps.

If your bread is slightly moist, you might want to lightly pre-toast the slices before assembling. To serve them as an appetizer or side, cut the slices in half before topping.

Look for a Gouda that is semisoft in texture but with the nuttiness that develops with age (ask your cheesemonger for suggestions!). Hard, aged varieties, although tasty, will not melt as well. This tartine will also be delicious with slightly funkier fontina, Taleggio, nutty Gruyère, or Comté.

Makes 4 tartines

1 Preheat the oven to 425°F [220°C]. Line a baking sheet with foil.

2 Heat a 12 in [30.5 cm] sauté pan or cast-iron skillet over medium-high heat. Add the oil and butter, and once the butter has melted, add the mushrooms. Cook, undisturbed, for 3 minutes, until the undersides brown. Continue to cook, stirring occasionally, until the liquid has evaporated and the mushrooms begin to brown, another 7 to 8 minutes. Stir in the garlic and thyme and cook for 1 minute. Add the wine and deglaze the pan, scraping the browned bits from the bottom of the pan, until the wine evaporates, 1 to 2 minutes. Remove from the heat and toss in the parsley. Season with salt and pepper and set aside.

3 Place the bread slices in an even layer on the prepared baking sheet. Spread butter on each slice, all the way to the edges, and repeat with a thin layer of mustard (about 1 tsp for each slice). Divide the mushrooms evenly among the bread slices (yes, use all of them!) and then top with the cheese. Press the cheese down slightly with your hand to make sure it sticks to the mushrooms. Sprinkle with flaky sea salt and black pepper.

4 Bake until the cheese is melty, 5 to 7 minutes. Turn the broiler on high and cook until the tops begin to brown, another 1 to 3 minutes. Garnish with chives and serve immediately.

1 Tbsp extra-virgin olive oil

1 Tbsp unsalted butter, plus more at room temperature for spreading

1½ lb [680 g] cremini mushrooms, stemmed and sliced

3 garlic cloves, cut into thin slices

1½ tsp fresh thyme leaves, minced

3 Tbsp white or red wine or dry sherry

2 Tbsp finely chopped fresh flat-leaf parsley

Kosher salt

Freshly ground black pepper

4 thick slices sturdy sourdough bread

1 Tbsp plus 1 tsp Dijon mustard

8 oz [230 g] young Gouda, coarsely grated (about 2 cups)

Flaky sea salt, for sprinkling

Fresh minced chives, for garnish

TUNA MELT

ON RYE

I wanted to breathe new life into the classic tuna melt. So, when the cheesemonger suggested dill Havarti, I had a lightbulb moment. Havarti is creamy and buttery as it is, but the addition of light, lemony dill makes it sing with flavor and aroma. Melted over the tuna salad, it elevates each bite, while tangy rye sourdough (further playing off the Scandinavian vibes here) cuts through the richness. As someone who never understood tuna melts, I now crave them around the clock.

I prefer dense and moist Scandinavian sourdough rye to the airy Jewish variety that's flecked with caraway seeds—but make this recipe with whatever is more available or appealing to you. If you can't find dill Havarti, use plain Havarti instead and add 2 Tbsp finely chopped fresh dill to the tuna salad. In the summertime, this open-faced sandwich would be delicious with a few juicy, ripe tomato slices tucked in.

Makes 4 open-faced sandwiches

1 Preheat the oven to 400°F [200°C]. Line a baking sheet with parchment paper or aluminum foil.

2 In a medium bowl, combine the tuna, mayonnaise, pickles, celery, onion, chives, lemon juice, and mustard. Season with the paprika, salt, and pepper.

3 Toast the bread slices.

4 Divide the salad evenly between the toasted bread slices and top with the cheese. Transfer to the prepared baking sheet and bake until the cheese is melty and the tuna has heated through, 5 to 8 minutes. Serve immediately.

Two 5 oz [140 g] cans tuna packed in water, drained

⅓ cup [80 g] mayonnaise

¼ cup [40 g] finely chopped bread-and-butter pickles or relish

3 Tbsp finely chopped celery (about 1 small stalk)

3 Tbsp finely chopped red onion

1½ Tbsp minced fresh chives

1 Tbsp fresh lemon juice (from about ½ medium lemon)

1½ Tbsp whole grain mustard

¼ tsp paprika, plus more as needed

Kosher salt

Freshly ground black pepper

4 slices rye bread

4 slices dill Havarti cheese

WELSH RAREBIT

While the story behind the name of Welsh rarebit, or rabbit, is long and complicated, its thick, savory cheese sauce flavored with mustard, Worcestershire, and beer (a classic British combination) comes together quickly. While it makes for a luscious topping for roasted vegetables and meat, more often it is smeared on toast and broiled until bubbling and brown—an instant hit wherever you are in the world. Look for a good-quality aged Cheddar that has a nice tang to it. As for the beer, Guinness or, even better, an oatmeal stout like Samuel Smith's will lend a rich maltiness that rounds out the salty sharpness of the cheese.

Makes 4 toasts

1 In a medium saucepan, melt the butter over medium heat. Whisk in the flour and cook until lightly brown, about 1 minute. Stir in the mustard, cayenne, and a big pinch of salt. Slowly pour in the stout and Worcestershire and cook, stirring all the while, until thickened, about 1 minute more. Lower the heat to medium-low and add the cheese gradually, stirring until melted and the mixture is fully combined—do not let the mixture come to a boil. Once smooth, season with more cayenne, Worcestershire, and salt, as desired. Remove from the heat. Pour into a shallow container and allow to set. Cooled, covered, and refrigerated, the sauce will last for up to 3 days.

2 When the cheese has set, position a rack in the upper third of the oven and turn the broiler on high. Line a baking sheet with aluminum foil.

3 Place the toasted bread on the prepared baking sheet. Spoon a very thick layer, about ¼ in [6 mm] thick, of sauce onto the toasts and broil until bubbling and browned, 2 to 3 minutes. Serve immediately.

1 Tbsp unsalted butter

1 Tbsp all-purpose flour

1 tsp English dry mustard

½ tsp cayenne pepper, plus more to taste

Kosher salt

⅓ cup [80 ml] stout

2 tsp Worcestershire sauce, plus more if desired

6 oz [170 g] sharp aged Cheddar cheese, coarsely grated (about 1½ cups)

4 thick slices sturdy bread, toasted

FRENCH ONION

SOUP

The French turned what essentially started out as rustic peasant food into a gloriously rich, deeply savory, and crave-worthy dish. Caramelized onions are turned into a flavorful, velvety-thick broth, which is then ladled into a bowl and topped with a bread slice and a generous layer of nutty, slightly sweet Gruyère. A broil in the oven results in a bubbling and browned cap of melted cheese that you must fight through to reach the delicious goodness below it. If that's not a stroke of genius on the French's part, I don't know what is!

If you have homemade beef stock on hand, this is the time to use it. If not, seek out the best variety you can find or substitute chicken stock. I like to use a blend of yellow and red onions along with shallots as the base to lend complexity.

Serves 4 to 6

1 In a large, heavy-bottomed pot, melt the butter over medium heat. Add the onions and stir until they're fully coated in butter. Cook, stirring occasionally, until the onions have softened and turned translucent, about 20 minutes.

2 Add the salt and sugar, increase the heat to medium-high, and cook, stirring frequently, until the onions have browned and are caramelized, another 25 to 30 minutes. While you stir, make sure to scrape up the browned bits from the bottom so that they don't burn.

3 Lower the heat to medium-low and add the sliced garlic. Cook for another 1 to 2 minutes. Pour in the wine and deglaze the pan, stirring to scrape up the browned bits from the bottom of the pot. Cook until the liquid has evaporated and the onions begin to dry out again, 3 to 4 minutes.

4 Stir in the flour and cook for another 3 minutes—the mixture will turn into a thick paste. Pour in 1 cup [240 ml] of the stock and stir to fully incorporate. Add the thyme, bay leaf,

-cont.

¼ cup [55 g] unsalted butter

3 lb [1.4 kg] mixed onions (such as yellow, red, and shallots), cut into ¼ in [6 mm] slices

½ tsp kosher salt, plus more as needed

½ tsp sugar

3 garlic cloves, 2 cut into thin slices and 1 halved

½ cup [120 ml] dry white wine

3 Tbsp all-purpose flour

4 cups [960 ml] store-bought or homemade beef stock or broth

2 large thyme sprigs

1 large fresh or dried bay leaf

Freshly ground black pepper

1 Tbsp cognac or dry sherry (optional)

4 to 6 baguette slices

4 to 6 oz [115 to 170 g] Gruyère, coarsely grated (1 to 1½ cups)

and remaining 3 cups [720 ml] of stock. Bring to a boil, then lower the heat and simmer for 30 minutes, until the broth thickens. Remove the bay leaf and thyme sprigs and season with salt and pepper. Add the cognac (if using), and continue to simmer. The soup can be stored in an airtight container in the refrigerator for up to 4 days.

5 While the soup is simmering, rub each baguette slice with the halved garlic clove and then toast the bread.

6 About 10 minutes before you're ready to serve, turn the broiler on high. Put four to six ovenproof bowls or large ramekins on a rimmed baking sheet. Ladle the soup into the bowls and top each with a baguette slice. Divide the cheese among the servings, covering both the toast and the soup. Carefully transfer to the oven and broil until the cheese has melted and begins to bubble and brown, 4 to 8 minutes. Serve immediately.

7 Alternatively, you can place the garlic-rubbed toasts in an even layer on a baking sheet, top with some of the cheese, and broil until the cheese has melted, 2 to 4 minutes. Top each bowl with a cheesy toast and sprinkle any remaining cheese on top.

TOMATO
AND FENNEL
SOUP
WITH GRILLED BLUE CHEESE CROUTONS

I've lost count of the number of people who have told me that this dish instantly transports them back to their childhood. This recipe is a grown-up version of the irresistible pair we all grew up with. Fennel and white wine provide a bit more complexity to the soup, while a pungent blue (something I would have never eaten as a child!) provides the gooey cheese element. Either way, the grilled cheese–turned–croutons never fail to make me feel like a kid.

Serves 4 to 6

1 In a large pot, heat the olive oil over medium heat. Add the onion, fennel, and a big pinch of salt and cook, stirring occasionally, until the onion and fennel soften and begin to brown, 10 to 12 minutes. Stir in the garlic, basil, and oregano and cook for another 2 to 3 minutes. Add the wine and deglaze the pan, stirring to scrape up the browned bits from the bottom of the pot. Cook until the liquid evaporates, about 2 minutes.

2 Stir in the stock, the tomatoes and their juices, a big pinch of sugar, and another big pinch of salt. Raise the heat to medium-high and cook until the liquid begins to boil, then turn the heat to low and simmer, uncovered, for 25 minutes.

3 Remove from the heat and purée using an immersion blender, or let cool until no longer steaming and purée in batches in a blender. Stir in the heavy cream and season with salt. If needed, add sugar until the soup loses its acidic tang. Return the soup to low heat and keep warm while you make the croutons. The soup can be made 4 or 5 days in advance and kept refrigerated in the pot or an airtight container.

4 **To make the croutons:** In a small bowl, mash the blue cheese into the cream cheese until incorporated

-cont.

3 Tbsp extra-virgin olive oil

1 medium yellow onion, cut into thin slices

1 fennel bulb, cut into thin slices

Kosher salt

3 garlic cloves, smashed

1 fresh basil sprig

1 fresh oregano sprig

¼ cup [60 ml] dry white wine

4 cups [950 ml] store-bought or homemade chicken or vegetable stock or broth

One 28 oz [795 g] can crushed tomatoes

Pinch of sugar, plus more as needed

¼ cup [60 ml] heavy cream

—

GRILLED BLUE CHEESE CROUTONS

4 oz [115 g] blue cheese, such as Gorgonzola or Danish blue (about 1 cup), crumbled

2 oz [60 g] cream cheese, at room temperature

Unsalted butter, at room temperature, for spreading

4 slices country white or sourdough bread

and spreadable. Butter each slice of bread on one side. Flip over and spread the blue cheese mixture evenly between the unbuttered sides of each slice. Place 2 slices on top of the other 2 slices, buttered-side up.

5 Heat a panini press or a large cast-iron or nonstick skillet over medium heat. If using a panini press, grill the sandwiches until the bread is golden and crispy and the cheese is melted, 4 to 5 minutes. If cooking in a pan, place both sandwiches inside the pan, cover with a lid, and let cook until the bottoms are browned, 3 to 4 minutes. Flip, turn the heat to medium-low, and continue to cook, covered, for 1 to 2 minutes more, until the other sides are also nicely browned and the cheese has melted.

6 Transfer to a cutting board and let sit for a minute before cutting into bite-size pieces. Immediately serve atop bowls of soup.

LET'S
GATHER
AROUND

IT'S A RACLETTE

PARTY!

For me, Raclette (also the term for the actual meal itself) exemplifies all the best hot cheese has to offer: layers of toasty, molten cheese straight from the wheel layered over starchy, briny fixings, creating a deeply comforting, satisfying, and exciting meal best shared with friends and family around the table. But while most of us don't have access to elaborate grill models or restaurants with master Swiss *racleurs*, that doesn't mean we can't re-create the magic of this Alpine *fromage* at home. Consider this your guide on all things Raclette—which wedge to choose, what to pair it with, and most importantly, how to gracefully cook and serve it. Eat, drink some white wine, and then repeat.

CHEESE

Traditionally, Raclette is produced in four different valleys in the Swiss Alpine region of Valais. That being said, there are number of good-quality Raclettes coming from the other side of the Alps in France and a few are even being made in the United States. Look for wheels that are semifirm, aged 3 to 6 months, and have a washed rind. The best are just as delicious snacked on as they are melted, so ask your cheesemonger to sample whatever they have on hand and choose which one tastes best to you—its flavors and aromas will only intensify and bloom with heat. When thinking of how much to buy, figure 4 to 6 oz [115 to 170 g] per person. Buying an extra portion or two in case of hearty appetites never hurts, either!

ACCOUTREMENTS

Boiled new or fingerling potatoes, cornichons, and pickled white pearl onions are a must. But as long as you have a starch, something briny, and even a cured meat or two, you can't go wrong. Here are other treats to consider:

Bread
Fresh crusty baguette, cubed sourdough

Vegetables
Boiled new potatoes; roasted Brussels sprouts, asparagus, broccoli; sautéed mushrooms; fresh tomatoes; potato chips

Pickles
Cornichons or dill pickles; pickled white pearl onions, carrots, green beans, cauliflower, mushrooms; marinated artichokes

Spice
White or black pepper, spicy Dijon mustard

Cured Meat
Italian bresaola (dried, cured beef), prosciutto, *jambon de Paris*, speck, smoked or hard salami like *saucisson sec* or soppressata, a nice pan-seared steak

Drink
Crisp white wine, kirsch or similar fruit brandy, herbal tea, and soda for the kids

EQUIPMENT

The most accessible and affordable are the flat-style grills that range from 2- to 8-person sets. Some require no electricity, slowly melting Raclette in *coupelles* or small trays set over tea lights. Others are a bit higher-tech, warming cheese below in trays, while the top grills veggies and meats. For those really serious about their Raclette, there are elaborate models that slant and cook entire half or quarter wheels from above. For those not ready to commit, there's always the DIY approach of a cast-iron skillet and a good broiler.

RACLETTE

~~~~~

As noted above, the traditional accompaniments to Raclette are new potatoes, cornichons, pickled white onions, and dried cured beef. However, feel free to pair your cheese with other vegetables (pickled or cooked) and cured meats and allow guests to experiment with different pairings throughout the night. When preparing, be sure to have all your ingredients arranged and ready to go before you begin melting and serving the cheese. Don't be tempted to remove the rind: A lot of the flavor is locked within those edges. Wrap any leftover cheese in parchment or wax paper, put it in an airtight container or zip-top bag, and refrigerate—it will keep for up to 5 weeks this way.

Serves 4 to 6

1 Put the potatoes in a large pot and cover with cold water. Salt generously and place over high heat. Bring to a boil, turn the heat to low, and simmer until fork tender, about 10 minutes. Drain, transfer back to the pot, cover, and keep warm until ready for serving.

2 Meanwhile, arrange the accompaniments and cheese on the table.

3 When ready to serve, if using a flat-style Raclette set, place 1 cheese slice into each *coupelle* or small tray. While the cheese is warming, have guests fill their plates with the warm potatoes and other accompaniments. When the cheese has melted and begins to bubble, remove the trays from the heat and scrape them using a mini spatula or fork over plates. Season with a pinch of pepper and Dijon mustard (if using) before eating. Repeat until you can't take another bite.

4 For a DIY approach, turn the broiler on high. Place the cheese slices in an even layer in a cast-iron or ovenproof skillet. Have guests fill their plates and place them either on the stovetop or by the oven. Cook the cheese under the broiler, watching constantly, for 1 to 2 minutes, or until the cheese begins to melt and sizzle but not brown. Remove from the heat and divide the cheese evenly among plates. Eat immediately and garnish the Raclette, as desired.

———

ACCOMPANIMENTS

2 to 2½ lb [910 g to 1.2 kg] small new or fingerling potatoes, unpeeled

1 to 1½ lb [455 to 680 g] thinly sliced cured meat, such as bresaola, ham, prosciutto, or salami, for serving

Cornichons or small dill pickles, for serving

Pickled white pearl onions, for serving

Roasted, blanched, or sautéed vegetables, such as Brussels sprouts, asparagus, or mushrooms, for serving (optional)

Pickled or marinated vegetables, such as carrots, green beans, and artichokes, for serving (optional)

Baguette or sourdough bread, cut into thin slices, for serving (optional)

—

1 to 1½ lb [455 to 680 g] Raclette, cut into ⅓ in [8 mm] thick slices

Freshly ground white or black pepper, for garnish

Dijon mustard, for garnish (optional)

FONDUE?

Fondue is a come one, come all type of deal. The kind that requires a bubbling pot of molten cheese, a spread of fruit, veggies, and bread (but really, anything goes), a hearty appetite, and a big-enough table to fit everyone around. Let guests dip away to their heart and stomach's content, and you ensure an effortlessly fun and memorable evening each and every time. While whole books have been written on fondue with hundreds of variations, for our purposes, we'll keep it simple and stick with classic Swiss—the one that started it all. Here's everything you need to know to do fondue.

CHEESE

The basic formula for fondue is melting cheese in white wine, along with garlic and kirsch (a cherry-distilled clear brandy) until it's a smooth, glossy dip. Nutty and sweet-salty Gruyère is almost always in the mix and is traditionally combined with either supple, buttery, mild Emmental (my go-to) or creamy washed-rind Vacherin Fribourgeois for complexity. Feel free to play around with a blend of other Alpine-style, low-moisture wedges like Appenzeller, Comté, Beaufort, Raclette, or Fontina Valle d'Aosta. Find the best quality you can afford—fondue is all about the cheese, after all.

WINE

Wine's purpose goes beyond providing flavor. Its acidity also helps break down proteins in the cheese and keeps them from clumping together and turning your lovely fondue into a stringy, lumpy, and/or broken mess. Seek out a dry acidic white wine, such as Sauvignon Blanc or Pinot Grigio—no need to buy anything fancy. To help keep the fondue beautifully emulsified, I also add a bit of lemon juice for acidity (its brightness also helps balance the fondue's richness).

ACCOUTREMENTS

Usually, the Swiss eat their fondue only with crusty bread (a must!), but feel free to add the following:

Vegetables
Boiled potatoes; blanched broccoli, cauliflower, Brussels sprouts, asparagus, or carrots; fresh cherry tomatoes or chopped bell peppers; cornichons

Fruit
Chopped apples or pears, grapes, or even pineapple

Meat
Smoked or hard salamis or sausages, cubed ham

Drink
Dry white wine, a shot of kirsch, or herbal tea to help with digestion. Not as traditional, but I think a farmhouse cider, Belgian-style ale, Pilsner, or any dry sparkling wine would also work well.

EQUIPMENT

Fondue pots are called *caquelon* and are either electric, ceramic, stainless steel, or cast iron. With electric, you have more control over the temperature. With the other three, you'll sometimes have to buy a separate Sterno flame, but it's easier to clean and you don't have to deal with any plugs. Either way, I find the easiest and most reliable way to get perfect fondue is to make it on the stovetop and transfer it to the fondue serving pot set over a low flame. Long, skinny dipping forks tend to accompany fondue sets but can be bought separately. Regular forks also work well.

-cont.

SWISS FONDUE

~~~~~~~~

I like my garlic a bit more pro-nounced, so I add it in minced. Traditionally, however, you simply halve a clove and rub the inside of your pot with the cut side before you add the wine.

Serves 4

1 In a large mixing bowl, toss the cheeses with the cornstarch to evenly coat. Set aside.

2 Add the wine, lemon juice, and garlic to a fondue pot or medium-heavy saucepan (prefer-ably enamel coated) and bring to a simmer over medium-low heat. Gradually begin to whisk in the cheese, one handful at a time. Stir constantly in a figure-eight motion to prevent the mixture from clumping and burning, adding more cheese as soon as the previous handful melts. Cook just until the cheese is melted, smooth, and glossy—don't let it come to a boil. Stir in the kirsch (if using) and nutmeg, until fully incorporated.

3 If not already in a fondue pot, transfer the mixture to a fondue pot set over a low flame to keep it warmed and melted at the table. Serve immediately with accoutrements. Once you finish the fondue, the hardened and browned cheese at the bottom of the pot is called *la religieuse* and is considered a delicacy.

————

8 oz [230 g] Gruyère, coarsely grated (2 cups), at room temperature

8 oz [230 g] Alpine-style good-quality cheese, such as Emmental, Comté, Raclette, or Vacherin Fribourgeois, coarsely grated (2 cups), at room temperature

1 Tbsp plus 1 tsp cornstarch

1 cup [240 ml] dry white wine, such as Sauvignon Blanc or Pinot Grigio

1 Tbsp fresh lemon juice (from about ½ medium lemon)

1 garlic clove, peeled and minced

1 Tbsp kirsch (optional)

Generous pinch of freshly grated nutmeg

TIPS & TRICKS

Here are a few tips to ensure a smooth, glossy fondue every time:

- **Grate or shred cheese to help make the melting process smooth and easier—a food processor makes quick work of this.**

- **Coating the cheese with corn-starch helps prevent clumps and ensure the fondue is stable and doesn't separate.**

- **Start with room-temperature cheese. Cold cheese into hot wine will cause it to ball up.**

- **Slowly incorporate handfuls of the cheese over a moderately low heat. This way, the cheese doesn't overheat and clump.**

- **Keep it warm once it's made. If it cools down too quickly before serving, it'll turn stringy and tough.**

- **And lastly, don't over-stir! Doing this will encourage stringiness. Once all the ingredients are fully incorporated, leave it alone.**

CHEESE DIP

While pimento cheese is perfect as is as a spread, it also makes a pretty darn good queso-like dip. This particular version is smooth and velvety and has a kick of smoke and heat thanks to chipotle in adobo sauce—even pimento purists will find it delicious. Also, big shout-out to J. Kenji López-Alt's method of using cornstarch and evaporated milk to make a smooth, velvety sauce that doesn't break or turn gritty—without the help of Velveeta or a béchamel!

I love serving this dip with Ritz Crackers, pretzels, and an assortment of veggies like bell peppers, carrots, and celery. To give this dip a queso twist, omit the mayonnaise, bump up the cornstarch to 1 Tbsp (mixing it with 1 Tbsp liquid for the slurry), and use one 12 fl oz [355 ml] can evaporated milk. Use leftover chipotle purée to flavor sauces, dips, marinades, soups, and stews.

Serves 4 to 6

1 To make the chipotle purée: Put the chipotle peppers and adobo sauce in a small food processor or blender and blend until the mixture turns into a smooth purée. Set aside. The chipotle purée can be made in advance, stored in an airtight container, and refrigerated for up to 2 months.

2 On a cutting board, sprinkle the garlic with a large pinch of salt and gather it into a small mound. Holding the blunt side of the knife with both hands, press and scrape the knife's sharp end, holding it at a slight angle, across the garlic mound to flatten it. Repeat, dragging it across the garlic, until you have a smooth paste. Set aside.

3 In a small bowl, mix the cornstarch and 1½ tsp of the evaporated milk into a slurry. Pour the rest of the evaporated milk into a medium saucepan and stir in the slurry. Bring to a boil over medium-high heat, whisking constantly. Turn the heat to low and

CHIPOTLE PEPPER PURÉE

One 7 oz [200 g] can chipotle in adobo sauce

—

½ garlic clove, minced

Kosher salt

1½ tsp cornstarch

One 5 fl oz [150 ml] can evaporated milk (about ½ cup plus 2 Tbsp)

8 oz [230 g] sharp or extra-sharp Cheddar cheese, coarsely grated (about 2 cups)

2 oz [55 g] cream cheese, roughly diced, at room temperature

¼ cup [60 g] mayonnaise

One 4 oz [115 g] jar diced pimento peppers, drained

add the Cheddar gradually by the handful, stirring until the Cheddar is melted and the mixture is smooth. Add the cream cheese and whisk until it melts. Stir in the mayonnaise, pimento peppers, 1½ tsp of the chipotle purée, and the garlic paste. Season with salt. Transfer to a serving bowl or keep it warm in a slow cooker and serve immediately.

4 To reheat the sauce, microwave it, stirring every 30 seconds, until fully melted.

BAKED BRIE

WITH PEAR-GINGER COMPOTE AND PEPPERY HAZELNUTS

When baked until melty and oozy, Brie begs to be spooned over a fresh crusty baguette. You'll find a nuanced pairing in the ginger-pear compote and layers of heat, flavor, and texture in the peppery hazelnuts.

Serves 4 to 6

1 **To make the compote:** In a small saucepan over medium heat, combine the honey, lemon juice, and ground ginger and bring to a simmer. Add the pear, crystallized ginger, and a big pinch of salt and cook, stirring frequently, until the pear softens and turns candy-like and the liquid mostly evaporates, about 10 minutes. Remove from the heat and set aside. This compote can be made up to 3 days in advance and kept refrigerated in an airtight container.

2 **To make the hazelnuts:** In a small skillet over medium heat, toss the hazelnuts with the olive oil and cook, stirring frequently, until golden and toasted, 3 to 4 minutes. If the hazelnut pieces begin to brown too quickly, turn the heat to medium-low. Transfer to a small bowl and, while the nuts are still warm, mix in the honey and vinegar. Season with salt and the black pepper (it might seem like a lot, but you want them to be very spicy to hold up to the cheese). Set aside. The nuts can be stored in an airtight container at room temperature up to 1 week in advance.

3 When ready to assemble, preheat the oven to 350°F [180°C].

4 Cut ten or twelve ½ in [1.25 cm] slits on the top of the Brie. Place the Brie in a Brie baker or a small shallow baking dish. Bake until the cheese has puffed up and feels melty inside when pressed with a finger, about 20 minutes.

5 Transfer to a serving board. Spoon the compote over the top and sprinkle with the hazelnuts. Drizzle with honey, grind more black pepper on top, and serve immediately with a fresh baguette, crostini, or crackers.

PEAR-GINGER COMPOTE

2 Tbsp honey

2 tsp fresh lemon juice

¼ tsp ground ginger

1 large Bosc pear, cut into medium dice

3 to 4 Tbsp finely chopped crystallized ginger

Kosher salt

—

PEPPERY HAZELNUTS

¼ cup [40 g] hazelnuts, chopped

1 tsp extra-virgin olive oil

½ tsp honey

¼ tsp white wine vinegar

Kosher salt

1 tsp freshly ground black pepper, plus more for sprinkling

—

8 oz [230 g] Brie wheel

Honey, for garnish

Freshly ground black pepper

Baguette, crostini, or crackers, for serving

CAMEMBERT EN CROÛTE

WITH QUICK SHALLOT-HONEY JAM

Nothing feels more special than digging into an entire wheel of Camembert—Brie's funkier and earthier bloomy-rind cousin—wrapped in flaky, buttery puff pastry and baked until melty and impossibly gooey. Making baked Camembert at home is not only easy with the help of store-bought pastry, but, because you can build and add flavor with fillings and toppings, you can tailor it to suit your tastes. Here, a quick shallot, honey, and thyme jam adds fantastic tang and brings the delectable centerpiece to a whole new sweet-and-savory level.

Serves 4 to 6

1 **To make the jam:** In a large skillet over medium heat, melt the butter. Add the shallots, thyme, and a big pinch of salt and cook for 8 to 10 minutes, or until the shallots soften and begin to brown. Stir in the vinegar, honey, and red pepper flakes and continue to cook, stirring constantly, until the honey-vinegar mixture begins to cling to the shallots, 2 to 3 minutes. Remove from the heat.

Season with salt and, if desired, more red pepper flakes. Set aside and let cool completely.

2 Preheat the oven to 375°F [190°C]. Line a baking sheet with parchment paper.

3 In a small bowl, combine the egg and heavy cream. Set aside.

4 On a clean work surface, lay down the pastry sheet. Spread half of the cooled shallot-honey jam in the center in a circle the size of the cheese wheel. Place the cheese wheel on top of it. Spread the remaining jam over the top.

5 Working quickly, gather up the edges of the dough, pressing around the cheese, and gather at the top. Pleat the upper edges to fit snugly around the cheese and squeeze the excess dough together to create somewhat of a topknot and to seal in the cheese. Trim excess dough if needed and tie the topknot together with a piece of kitchen twine to hold the pleats together

SHALLOT-HONEY JAM

1 Tbsp unsalted butter

4 large shallots, cut into thin slices (about 2 cups [200 g])

2 tsp minced fresh thyme, plus more for garnish

Kosher salt

2 Tbsp white wine vinegar

1 Tbsp honey

¼ tsp red pepper flakes, or more if desired

—

1 egg, lightly beaten

1 Tbsp heavy cream, whole milk, or water

1 frozen puff pastry sheet, thawed but chilled

8 oz [230 g] Camembert or Brie wheel, chilled

½ tsp minced fresh thyme

Flaky sea salt

and prevent breakage. Refrigerate for 15 to 20 minutes, or until the pastry is chilled and firm to the touch. The assembled, unbrushed cheese wheel can be made up to 2 weeks in advance: Simply wrap in plastic wrap and freeze until ready to bake, allowing an extra 5 to 10 minutes in the oven.

6 Transfer the cheese wheel to the prepared baking sheet. Remove the kitchen twine. Brush the pastry evenly with the egg wash and sprinkle with the thyme and flaky sea salt.

7 Bake until the pastry is golden brown and firm to the touch all over, 40 to 50 minutes. Remove from the oven and let the baked cheese sit for 10 to 15 minutes at room temperature. Transfer to a plate and serve.

ASPARAGUS, TALEGGIO, AND PRESERVED
LEMON TART

1 frozen puff pastry sheet, thawed but chilled

6 to 8 oz [170 to 225 g] Taleggio cheese, cold

3 Tbsp fresh tarragon leaves

2 Tbsp finely chopped preserved lemon (see headnote)

10 oz [280 g] asparagus (preferably pencil-thin), woody ends trimmed

2 tsp extra-virgin olive oil

Freshly ground black pepper

1 egg, lightly beaten

1 Tbsp heavy cream, milk, or water

A puff pastry tart is a great party trick because you can throw it together at the last minute with whatever vegetable, cheese, or spread you have. It feeds a crowd and is always a hit. This stunning and appetizing version spotlights both Taleggio—an Italian semisoft washed-rind (read: funky) cow's milk cheese—and springtime asparagus, while preserved lemon and fresh tarragon help brighten and balance the richness. It's a bold marriage of flavors, but nestled into buttery, flaky pastry, it totally works.

If your asparagus is on the thicker side, cut the spears in half lengthwise before arranging them on the tart. Preserved lemon can be substituted with the zest of 1 lemon, used as a garnish at the end.

Serves 4 to 6

1 Preheat the oven to 400°F [200°C]. Either butter a large baking sheet or line it with parchment paper.

2 On a lightly floured surface, roll out the pastry sheet to an 11 by 14 in [28 by 35.5 cm] rectangle and transfer to the prepared baking sheet. Using a sharp knife, score a smaller rectangle ½ in [12 mm] from the edges. Prick the inside of the marked rectangle all over with a fork.

3 Cut the Taleggio into thin slices and then tear each slice into two pieces. Evenly distribute the Taleggio within the marked rectangle. Top with 2 Tbsp of the tarragon leaves and the preserved lemon. Arrange the asparagus on the tart so that they fit crosswise—if the spears are too long, trim them—and brush with the olive oil. Season with black pepper. Transfer the baking sheet to the refrigerator or freezer to chill the dough, 5 to 10 minutes.

4 In a small bowl, combine the egg with the cream and brush the edges of the tart with the egg wash.

5 Bake the tart for 18 to 22 minutes, or until the pastry is golden brown and crisp. Let sit for 5 to 10 minutes before garnishing with the remaining 1 Tbsp of tarragon and serving.

BEST
NACHOS
IN THE WORLD

Nachos are one of my favorite foods, and over the years, I've pinned down what makes the best nachos in the world—*for me*. Blue over yellow corn chips, red over yellow onions, plenty of sharp Cheddar, chèvre for creamy tang, pickled jalapeños for heat *and* acidity, no meat (just well-seasoned beans), and lime-kissed radishes, avocado, and bright green cilantro to finish. But I'm a firm believer that nachos should really be a no-recipe recipe. Use this one as your starting point and play around with it until you, too, find your own version of "best." If you're feeling more of a queso on your nachos (in which case, omit the cheeses listed and don't bake), I recommend using a thinned version of the Hot Pimento Cheese Dip (page 64).

I include a recipe for quick-seasoned beans, but feel free to substitute refried beans instead (I like Annie's brand!). If you want to try your hand at pickling jalapeños, you'll find a recipe here for that, too.

Serves 4 to 6

1 Preheat the oven to 350°F [180°C]. Oil a large baking sheet.

2 In a small bowl, toss the radish slices with the lime juice and set aside.

3 **To make the beans:** In a skillet, heat the oil over medium-low heat. Add the garlic and cook until fragrant, about 1 minute. Increase the heat to medium and add the beans, cumin, coriander, and a big pinch of salt. Toss to coat and cook, stirring frequently, until the beans are warmed through, about 2 minutes. Remove from the heat and set aside.

4 Spread half of the tortilla chips out on the baking sheet. Top with half of the beans, the onion, jalapeños, one-third of the chévre, and half of the grated cheese, in that order. Repeat the layers with the remaining beans, onion, jalapeños, another third of the chévre, and the remaining grated cheese.

-cont.

3 or 4 radishes, cut into thin slices

1 Tbsp fresh lime juice

—

CUMIN-CORIANDER BEANS

1 Tbsp extra-virgin olive oil

1 garlic clove, minced

One 15 oz [425 g] can black or pinto beans, rinsed and drained

1 tsp ground cumin

½ tsp ground coriander

Pinch of kosher salt

—

One 16 oz [455 g] bag blue corn tortilla chips

½ medium red onion, diced, or Lime-Pickled Red Onions (page 96)

2 Pickled Jalapeño Peppers (recipe follows), or 1 fresh jalapeño pepper, cut into thin slices

6 oz [170 g] chèvre, crumbled

8 oz [230 g] coarsely grated sharp Cheddar cheese, Monterey Jack cheese, or a combination of both (2 cups)

1 avocado, cut into slices, for garnish

Fresh cilantro leaves, for garnish

Sour cream, for serving

Pico de gallo or red salsa, for serving

Tomatillo Salsa Verde (page 87), for serving

Hot sauce, for topping

5 Bake until the cheese is melted, 20 to 25 minutes. Garnish with avocado slices, the remaining chèvre, the radish slices, and cilantro. Serve immediately with sour cream, salsas, and hot sauce.

PICKLED JALAPEÑO PEPPERS

This easy, quick pickle tames jalapeño's kick (just a bit!) while introducing an acidity that I simply find addictive. Put pickled jalapeño into any recipe where you want heat and brightness. Kept in brine and chilled, these will keep for up to 2 months.

Makes 1 pint [475 ml]

1 Put the garlic in a small bowl or a 2 cup [480 ml] liquid measuring container and top with the jalapeño slices.

2 In a small saucepan, stir together ½ cup [120 ml] of water, the vinegar, sugar, and salt and bring to a boil over medium-high heat. Cook, stirring, for 1 to 2 minutes, until the sugar and salt are dissolved.

3 Remove from the heat and immediately pour the pickling liquid over the jalapeños. If the jalapeños aren't fully submerged, top with a ramekin to weight them down. Let cool completely at room temperature before transferring the jalapeños, garlic, and pickling liquid to a jar with a lid.

4 Cover and refrigerate for 3 hours before using. Pickled jalapeños can be stored in an airtight container in the refrigerator for up to 2 months.

———

1 garlic clove

About 10 large jalapeño peppers, cut into ⅛ in [4 mm] slices

½ cup [120 ml] white or apple cider vinegar

¼ cup [50 g] sugar

1 Tbsp kosher salt

HAMA HAMA SMOKED

OYSTER DIP

After a night of camping on the Olympic Peninsula and basking in spring's warm air, my friends and I were hungry and ready to feast at Hama Hama Oyster Saloon right on Hood Canal. We readily slurped down fresh and grilled oysters, but the meal's real sleeper hit was the hot and cheesy smoked oyster dip. We devoured it within minutes of its arrival at our table and even contemplated ordering a second. Big thanks to Hama Hama's owner, Lissa James Monberg, for letting us re-create the magic at home with her recipe!

If you can get your hands on fresh smoked oysters (you can order Hama Hama's on their website, www.hamahamaoysters .com), that will be best, but you'll find success with the canned variety as well.

Serves 4 to 6

1 Preheat the oven to 400°F [200°C].

2 On a cutting board, sprinkle the garlic with a large pinch of salt and gather it into a small mound. Holding the blunt side of the knife with both hands, press and scrape the knife's sharp end, holding it at a slight angle, across the garlic mound to flatten it. Repeat, dragging it across the garlic, until you have a smooth paste. Set aside.

3 In the bowl of a stand mixer or a large mixing bowl, mix the cream cheese, sour cream, and Cheddar on medium speed until smooth, 2 to 3 minutes. Scrape down the sides of the bowl and add the Dijon, 1 tsp of salt, the black pepper, paprika, cumin, and a pinch of cayenne. Mix to incorporate. Add the garlic paste and chopped oysters and mix until combined.

4 Transfer to a 7 by 11 in [17 by 28 cm] baking dish or 10 in [25 cm] oven-proof skillet and sprinkle with Parmesan and cayenne. Bake until the dip is hot and bubbly, 15 to 20 minutes. Serve immediately with crostini, a baguette, or crackers.

2 garlic cloves

Kosher salt

One 8 oz [230 g] package cream cheese, at room temperature

1 cup plus 2 Tbsp [270 g] sour cream

7 oz [200 g] sharp Cheddar cheese, coarsely grated (about 1¾ cups)

1 tsp Dijon mustard

Heaping ¼ tsp freshly ground black pepper

Heaping ¼ tsp smoked paprika

⅛ tsp ground cumin

Pinch of cayenne pepper, plus more for sprinkling

4 oz [115 g] smoked oysters (from two 3 oz [85 g] cans), drained and roughly chopped

Freshly grated Parmesan cheese, for sprinkling

Crostini, baguette, or crackers, for serving

STARRING
MAINS

ADJARULI

KHACHA-PURI

It's no surprise that *khachapuri* (*khacha* for "cheese," *puri* for "bread") is Georgia's most beloved dish. Every region has its own version, and this particular cheese-carb wonder comes from Adjara, near the Black Sea. Whereas its shape is obviously a boat, you might not guess that its molten filling symbolizes the sea and the egg yolk the sun. Traditionally, this yeast bread is filled with stretchy Sulguni cheese and fresh Imeruli curds. To approximate these wheels, I use a combination of low-moisture whole milk mozzarella, briny feta, and creamy ricotta.

Makes 3 cheese breads

1 **To make the dough:** In a medium bowl, combine the flour, salt, sugar, and yeast. Make a well and add 1 cup plus 1 Tbsp [255 ml] of warm water (110 to 115°F [43 to 46°C]) and the oil. Start out mixing with a wooden spoon, then switch to using your hands to knead the dough into one shaggy mass. Cover with a clean, damp kitchen towel and let sit for 5 to 10 minutes to let the gluten relax (it'll make kneading it easier).

2 Transfer the dough to a lightly floured surface and knead it until the dough is soft and tender but elastic (a good test is to pinch the dough, and then pinch your earlobe—you want it softer than your ear). If the dough turned out too wet, add a bit more flour; if it's too dense, add a bit more water.

3 Once done, pour some oil into your hand and grease the sides of a large mixing bowl. Put the dough inside the bowl, form it into a ball, and pat the top of it to grease. Cover with a damp kitchen towel and set aside to rest in a warm place for about 1 hour, or until the dough has doubled in size.

4 Carefully grab an edge of the dough and stretch it over itself toward the opposite side. Repeat with the remaining edges. Transfer the dough to a lightly floured surface, divide it into three equal pieces, and form each into a little ball. Put on a lightly floured large plate or baking sheet and let rest for another 15 to 20 minutes.

DOUGH

2½ cups [350 g] all-purpose flour, plus more as needed

1 tsp kosher salt

1 tsp sugar

1 tsp instant (fast-acting) yeast

3 Tbsp sunflower or vegetable oil

—

FILLING

12 oz [340 g] low-moisture whole milk mozzarella, coarsely grated (about 3 cups)

3 oz [85 g] crumbled feta (about ⅔ cup)

3 oz [85 g] whole milk ricotta cheese (about ⅓ cup)

1 egg

1 tsp all-purpose flour

—

3 eggs

3 Tbsp unsalted butter

5 **Meanwhile, to make the filling:** In a medium bowl, mix the cheeses, egg, flour, and 1 Tbsp of water until thoroughly hydrated and combined. Divide into three sturdy balls and set aside.

-cont.

6 To assemble: Put an overturned rimmed baking sheet or pizza stone inside the oven and preheat it to 450°F [230°C]. Tear foil into three 5 by 8 in [12 by 20 cm] pieces. Set aside.

7 Crack each egg into a separate small bowl.

8 Punch down the dough again and transfer it to a well-floured surface. Take one piece, keeping the other two covered, and round it out gently with your fingers into a 4 to 5 in [10 to 12 cm] circle. Using a rolling pin, gently roll it out to an 8 in [20 cm] circle. Ideally, the sides will be thicker than the center. Take one edge of the circle and tightly roll it toward the center, about two-thirds of the way. Repeat with the opposite side. Pinch each end tightly together, pulling outward as you do, and pinch again to seal. Remember that you are creating a boat shape here.

9 Lightly flour one of the foil squares and place the formed dough on top of it. Take one of the cheese balls, place it in the center of the cavity, and press it down lightly to spread and pack it evenly throughout the center. Repeat the process with the remaining pieces of dough and cheese balls.

10 Carefully remove the baking sheet from the oven (don't do this if using a pizza stone). Holding on to the edges of the foil, transfer the khachapuri to the baking sheet (or pizza stone). I can usually get two khachapuri to fit on one sheet.

11 Bake in the oven until the dough is lightly golden brown and the cheese is melted, 8 to 9 minutes. Remove from the oven and, working with one khacha-puri at a time, carefully make a well in the cheese with a fork and slide an egg into it, being careful not to break the yolk. Return to the oven and finish baking until the egg whites have set and the khachapuri is a deep golden brown, another 3 to 5 minutes.

12 Remove the cheese breads and place each on a serv-ing plate. Top each with 1 Tbsp of the butter. Serve immediately.

RADICCHIO, FENNEL, FONTINA, AND CHÈVRE PIZZA

This pizza marries all my favorite ingredients. Nutty and mushroomy fontina is matched with creamy chèvre's fresh tang, while sautéed fennel provides a punch of flavor and slightly charred radicchio adds crunch (the oven heat tempers its bitter edge). This foolproof skillet method has become my go-to way to cook pizza and is adapted from *Josey Baker Bread* via my very talented chef-instructor friend Amanda Coba.

Makes 2 pizzas

1 Remove the dough from the refrigerator. Divide the dough into two equal pieces, shape into rounds, and transfer to a well-floured large plate or small baking sheet, leaving plenty of room between the dough pieces. Dust with more flour and lightly cover with plastic wrap or a damp kitchen towel. Let the dough sit until it comes to room temperature, 60 to 90 minutes.

2 Meanwhile, position a rack in the upper third of the oven. Turn the broiler on high and preheat for 30 minutes.

3 Heat the olive oil in a skillet over medium heat. Add the fennel and a big pinch of salt and cook, stirring frequently, until it softens and browns, 5 to 8 minutes. Add the garlic and cook for another minute. Pour in the wine and deglaze the pan, stirring to scrape up the browned bits from the bottom of the pan. Cook until the liquid evaporates, 1 to 2 minutes. Remove from the heat and season with salt and red pepper flakes. Set aside and have the rest of your toppings ready to go.

4 When ready to bake, heat a 10 to 12 in [25 to 30 cm] cast-iron or ovenproof skillet over medium-high heat for 3 to 5 minutes. Meanwhile, transfer one dough round to a well-floured surface, keeping the other

-cont.

1 lb [445 g] homemade or store-bought pizza dough

1 Tbsp extra-virgin olive oil, plus more for drizzling

1 fennel bulb, cut into thin slices

Kosher salt

2 or 3 garlic cloves, cut into ⅓ in [8 mm] slices

2 Tbsp dry white wine

Red pepper flakes

6 oz [170 g] good-quality fontina (Valle d'Aosta if you can find it), coarsely grated (1½ cups)

4 oz [115 g] chèvre, broken into pinch-size pieces

½ head radicchio (about 4 oz [115 g]), cored and cut into ½ in [12 mm] slices

Freshly grated Parmesan cheese, for garnish (optional)

Fennel fronds, for garnish

covered. Lightly dust the dough with flour and gently work the dough, pressing from the inside out and stretching, into a 10 to 12 in [25 to 30.5 cm] round. Dust with more flour if the dough starts to become sticky at any point.

5 Carefully transfer to the hot skillet, using your fingers or shaking the skillet to carefully arrange it into place.

6 Top it with half the fontina, leaving a ¾ to 1 in [2 to 2.5 cm] border. Spread half of the prepared fennel in an even layer and top with half of the chèvre. Continue to cook over medium-high heat until the bottom starts to develop brown spots all around (use a spatula to lift up the edges to check), anywhere from 1 to 4 minutes.

7 Carefully transfer the skillet to the oven and broil, rotating the pan halfway through to ensure even cooking, until the edges are puffed and lightly brown, 2 to 4 minutes.

8 Remove the pizza from the oven. Working quickly, top with half of the radicchio. Drizzle with olive oil and lightly sprinkle with salt. Return it to the oven and continue cooking for another 1 to 2 minutes, until the edges are lightly charred, the bottom is crisp, and the radicchio has wilted and begun to brown.

9 Remove the pizza from the skillet and transfer to a cutting board. Garnish with Parmesan (if using) and fennel fronds. Slice and serve immediately. Meanwhile, repeat the process to make a second pizza.

SPINACH, ARTICHOKE, AND LEEK
LASAGNA

This dish takes everything you know and love about a spinach and artichoke dip and turns it into a glorified white lasagna featuring layers of pasta; cheesy sauce fragrant with sautéed leeks, garlic, and a hint of nutmeg; ricotta flecked with spinach and Parmesan; and tangy marinated artichokes. It doesn't get better than this! I recommend using the best-quality ricotta you can find.

Serves 4 to 6

1 Preheat the oven to 350°F [180°C]. Butter or oil a 9 by 13 in [23 by 33 cm] baking dish.

2 In a large pot or saucepan, melt 1 Tbsp of the butter over medium heat. Add 1 bunch of spinach leaves and toss to coat with butter. Once the spinach has wilted down, add the second bunch. Cook until all the spinach leaves have wilted and are tender—the whole process should take 3 to 4 minutes. Transfer to a medium bowl. Once the spinach has cooled, discard any liquid at the bottom of the bowl and, working in handfuls, squeeze the excess moisture out.

Add the ricotta, Parmesan, and eggs and mix to combine. Season with salt and pepper and set aside.

3 In the same pot, melt the remaining 4 Tbsp [55 g] of butter over medium-low heat. Add the leek and a big pinch of salt and cook until the leek becomes tender, 5 to 6 minutes. Stir in the garlic and cook for another 2 minutes. Add the flour, stir to incorporate, and cook for 3 minutes, until the raw flour flavor cooks out. Use a whisk to stir in all the milk and then the broth a little bit at a time, waiting until the leek-flour mixture absorbs the liquid before pouring in more. Turn the heat to medium-high and bring the mixture to a boil, whisking occasionally. Lower the heat and simmer, whisking occasionally, for 5 minutes to thicken slightly. Over low heat, stir in the mozzarella, one handful at a time. Season with salt, pepper, and a big pinch of nutmeg.

5 Tbsp [70 g] unsalted butter

2 bunches spinach (about 10 oz [285 g] each), stemmed and chopped

1 lb [455 g] whole milk ricotta

4 oz [115 g] fresh Parmesan cheese, medium grated (1⅓ cups), plus more for garnishing

2 eggs, lightly beaten

Kosher salt

Freshly ground black pepper

1 large leek, washed thoroughly (see Note, page 118), dark green top removed, and cut into thin slices

4 garlic cloves, minced

¼ cup [35 g] flour

2 cups [480 ml] whole milk or half-and-half

2 cups [480 ml] chicken or vegetable stock or broth

8 oz [230 g] low-moisture whole milk mozzarella, coarsely grated (2 cups)

Freshly ground nutmeg

One 1 lb [455 g] box no-boil lasagna

One 14 oz [400 g] jar marinated artichokes, coarsely chopped

4 To assemble the lasagna, spread a quarter of the cheese sauce in an even layer on the bottom of the baking dish. Arrange 3 or 4 lasagna noodles in an even layer, breaking the noodles to fit as needed. Gently spread half of the ricotta mixture on top, followed by another quarter of the cheese sauce and half of the artichokes. Place another 3 or 4 noodles on top and then top with the remaining ricotta mixture, another quarter of the cheese sauce, and the remaining artichokes. Add another layer of 3 or 4 lasagna noodles and pour the remaining cheese sauce over the top. Top with Parmesan cheese (about ½ cup or 1½ oz [40 g]). Bake uncovered for 45 to 50 minutes or until the top has lightly browned and the juices are bubbling around the edges. Let the lasagna sit for at least 10 to 15 minutes before serving.

BLACK BEAN, CORN, AND ZUCCHINI

CHILES RELLENOS

WITH TOMATILLO SALSA VERDE

8 poblano peppers

1 Tbsp extra-virgin olive oil

1 medium red onion, chopped

Kosher salt

2 garlic cloves, minced

1½ tsp ground coriander

¾ tsp dried oregano

1 lb [455 g] zucchini, cut into medium dice (about 2 medium zucchini)

1 cup [140 g] frozen or fresh corn kernels (about 1½ ears)

One 15 oz [425 g] can black beans, drained and rinsed

4½ oz [130 g] crumbled queso fresco (¾ cup)

6 oz [170 g] Monterey Jack cheese, coarsely grated (about 1½ cups)

Tomatillo Salsa Verde (recipe follows), for serving

While chiles rellenos (roasted and stuffed poblano peppers) are typically battered and fried, I break with tradition and bake them instead to save time and to keep the dish light. If anything, baking allows the pepper's subtle heat and spice to better shine—especially in contrast to the sweet coriander and oregano–laced filling of sautéed red onions, corn, and zucchini. Black beans are thrown in for heft, along with queso fresco that turns ricotta-like in the oven, melding the flavors together. Last but not least is the "seal" of melted Monterey Jack, pushing these chiles rellenos into gooey hot cheese territory.

Serves 4 to 6

1 Place a rack in the upper third of the oven and turn the broiler on high. Line a baking sheet with aluminum foil.

2 Put the peppers on the prepared baking sheet. Broil, flipping halfway through with tongs, until the peppers are blackened, about 5 minutes on each side. Transfer to a large bowl and cover in plastic wrap. Let steam for 5 to 10 minutes.

3 When the peppers are steamed, peel off the blackened skins. Cut a slit down the side of each pepper, from right under the stem to the tip. Without ripping the peppers, carefully remove the seeds—you want the stem to remain intact. Transfer to a 9 by 13 in [23 by 33 cm] baking dish (you will have to squeeze them in to fit, or you can use a second, smaller dish) and let cool while you make the filling.

4 Preheat the oven to 350°F [180°C].

5 Heat the oil in a large skillet over medium heat. Add the onion and a pinch of salt and cook for 4 to 5 minutes, until the onion begins to soften. Add the garlic, coriander, and oregano and cook for 1 minute more. Stir in the zucchini and corn and cook for another 5 to 6 minutes, until the zucchini softens.

6 Transfer to a large bowl and let cool slightly. Stir in the black beans and queso fresco. Season with salt.

7 Fill each pepper with ½ cup [85 g] filling. Divide the Monterey Jack among the peppers, adding it in an even layer on top of each slit. The peppers can be made up to 1 day in advance and refrigerated.

8 Bake in the oven until the cheese melts, about 10 minutes. Serve immediately with tomatillo salsa verde for topping.

TOMATILLO SALSA VERDE

〜〜〜

Although a tomato-based sauce is a more traditional accompaniment to chiles rellenos, I love the kiss of tang this salsa verde provides. The best part is that it's incredibly easy to make!

Makes about 1½ cups [360 ml]

1 Position a rack in the upper third of the oven and turn on the broiler. Line a baking sheet with aluminum foil.

2 Place the tomatillos cut-side down in an even layer on the baking sheet. Broil for 5 to 10 minutes, or until the skins are lightly blackened.

3 Transfer the cooked tomatillos (no need to cool) to a food processor or blender. Add the onion, cilantro, jalapeño, garlic, and lime juice. Pulse until everything is finely chopped and incorporated. Season with salt.

4 Transfer to a serving bowl and refrigerate until completely cool before serving.

———

1 lb [455 g] tomatillos, husked, rinsed, and halved crosswise

½ cup [70 g] diced yellow onion

¼ cup [10 g] roughly chopped fresh cilantro leaves

1 jalapeño or serrano pepper, stemmed, seeded, and roughly chopped

1 large garlic clove

2 Tbsp fresh lime juice

Kosher salt

ROASTED BROCCOLI, RED ONION, AND DOUBLE

CHEDDAR GALETTE

I have been writing about the wonders of galettes, a rustic free-form tart, for years now. They're half the work of pies, yet they're just as impressive *and* delicious. This one features a match made in curd heaven—broccoli with a hint of char and melty sharp Cheddar—along with striking red onions that provide a savory sweetness to each bite. And because there's no such thing as too much cheese, I add it to both the filling *and* the crust, hence the double Cheddar!

Galettes are adaptable as well, so feel free to substitute whatever cooked vegetables or meats you have on hand. Instead of Cheddar, spring for another semifirm cheese with a low-moisture content, such as Parmesan, aged Gouda, or Alpine styles like Gruyère or Comté. You can also easily double or triple the pastry crust to meet all your cheesy-galette needs.

Makes one 12 in [30.5 cm] galette

1 **To make the pastry crust:** Mix the sour cream into ¼ cup [60 ml] of cold water and refrigerate until needed. In a large bowl, whisk together the flour, sugar, and salt. Add the cubed butter and toss to coat. With a fork or pastry cutter, cut the butter into the flour until it's the size of peas. Add the grated cheese and mix to combine with a rubber spatula.

2 Drizzle the sour cream mixture a few tablespoons at a time over the flour-butter mixture, using a spatula to incorporate. Continue to add more water, a few tablespoons at a time, until the dough is hydrated but not sticky—when you squeeze the dough, it shouldn't fall apart. If needed, add more water, a little bit at a time, until you reach this consistency.

3 Press the dough together and form into a disk about 4 in [10 cm] across by 1½ in [4 cm] thick. Wrap in plastic wrap and chill in the refrigerator

-cont.

CHEDDAR PASTRY CRUST

2 Tbsp cold sour cream or buttermilk

1¼ cups [175 g] all-purpose flour

1 tsp sugar

½ tsp kosher salt

½ cup [110 g] cold unsalted butter, cubed

1½ oz [40 g] coarsely grated sharp Cheddar cheese

—

FILLING

2 small broccoli heads (about 12 oz total [340 g]), cut into slices lengthwise, stem and all

1 small red onion, cut into 1 in [2.5 cm] segments

2 garlic cloves, cut into thin slices

1½ Tbsp extra-virgin olive oil

1½ tsp cumin seeds

1 tsp paprika

1 tsp kosher salt

—

¼ cup [60 g] sour cream

5 oz [140 g] sharp Cheddar cheese, coarsely grated (about 1¼ cups)

Freshly ground black pepper

1 egg, lightly beaten

1 Tbsp heavy cream, milk, or water

for at least 1 hour before using, or ideally overnight. The dough can be made in advance and kept refrigerated for up to 3 days or frozen for up to 3 months.

4 When ready to assemble the galette, preheat the oven to 400°F [200°C]. Line a baking sheet with parchment paper.

5 On a lightly floured surface, roll out the dough into a 14 in [35.5 cm] circle and carefully transfer to the prepared baking sheet. Refrigerate while you prepare the filling.

6 **To make the filling:** In a large bowl, combine the broccoli, red onion, garlic, olive oil, cumin, paprika, and salt. Spread out onto a large rimmed baking sheet in an even layer. Bake for 10 to 12 minutes, or until the broccoli is bright green and beginning to char at the edges but isn't completely cooked through. Let cool.

7 Once the filling has cooled completely, remove the dough from the refrigerator. Spread the sour cream evenly over the dough, leaving a 1½ in [4 cm] border all around. Sprinkle ¼ cup (1 oz [30 g]) of the Cheddar on top. Arrange the filling over the sour cream in an even layer—making sure the red onion segments are lying flat and not sticking up, or they'll burn. Top with ¾ cup [60 g] of cheese and a few cracks of black pepper. Fold the edges up and over the vegetables, pleating at points to make a circle. Refrigerate for 20 to 30 minutes (or 15 minutes in the freezer) to firm up the dough.

8 While the galette is chilling, preheat the oven to 400°F [200°C] if not already on.

9 In a small bowl, combine the egg and heavy cream. When ready to bake, brush the edges of the dough with the egg wash and sprinkle all over with the remaining ¼ cup [20 g] cheese and more black pepper. Bake until the galette is golden brown and crisp, 30 to 40 minutes. Serve while still warm.

CURRIED CAULIFLOWER AND FARRO

SKILLET BAKE

Curried cauliflower and whole grain farro marry together in this skillet bake with creamy ricotta, funky fontina, sharp Parmesan, and toasted bread crumbs. The result is curried, cheesy, and crispy . . . what more can you ask for in a veggie-grain dish that doesn't skimp on flavor—or fiber, for that matter? I cook most often with Madras curry powder, which includes cayenne for a bit of kick. If you can't find this specific blend, feel free to add cayenne, to taste, along with the other spices to mimic its fieriness.

Serves 4 to 6

1 Bring a large pot of water to a boil. Generously salt the water and add the farro. Cook until al dente, 25 to 30 minutes. Drain and set aside. The farro can be cooled, covered, and refrigerated for up to 3 days.

2 Meanwhile, use your hands to break the cauliflower into smaller florets and cut the stems into bite-size pieces. It's OK if the pieces crumble. Set aside.

3 Preheat the oven to 400°F [200°C].

4 Heat 2 Tbsp of the oil in a 12 in [30.5 cm] ovenproof skillet or a large heavy-bottomed pot over medium-low heat. Add the red onion, garlic, and a big pinch of salt and cook, stirring occasionally, until the onion softens, 7 to 8 minutes. Stir in the curry powder and fennel seeds and let the spices bloom (allowing their flavors to open up and deepen) for 1 minute more.

5 Add the cauliflower and a big pinch of salt. Using your spoon or spatula, and starting from the bottom of the pan and carefully working your way up, gently toss the cauliflower in the onion mixture. If you are cooking in a large pot, this will be a bit easier. Once it's fully coated and mixed in with the aromatics, continue to cook, stirring frequently over medium-low heat, until the cauliflower loses its raw bite, 7 to 8 minutes. Remove from the heat and transfer to a large mixing bowl. Keep the skillet nearby or

-cont.

Kosher salt

1 cup [180 g] farro, rinsed and drained

1 medium head cauliflower (about 2 lb [910 g]), cut lengthwise into ½ in [12 mm] slices (green leaves and stems included)

3 Tbsp extra-virgin olive oil

1 large red onion, chopped

3 garlic cloves, cut into thin slices

1½ Tbsp Madras curry powder

1 tsp fennel or cumin seeds, crushed

1 Tbsp lemon zest (from about 1 large lemon)

8½ oz [240 g] ricotta cheese (1 cup)

8 oz [230 g] good-quality fontina (Valle d'Aosta if you can find it), coarsely grated (2 cups)

2 oz [55 g] fresh Parmesan cheese, coarsely grated (½ cup)

½ cup [30 g] panko bread crumbs

2 Tbsp finely chopped fresh flat-leaf parsley

prepare a 9 by 13 in [23 by 33 cm] baking dish by buttering or oiling it.

6 Add the drained farro and lemon zest to the cauliflower mixture and stir to combine. Stir in the ricotta, fontina, and half of the Parmesan. Season with salt. Transfer to the skillet or baking dish and spread into an even layer. The dish can be made, covered, and refrigerated 1 day in advance before baking.

7 In a small bowl, mix the bread crumbs with the parsley, remaining Parmesan, and remaining 1 Tbsp of oil until evenly mixed and the bread crumbs are saturated with the oil. Sprinkle over the cauliflower and farro.

8 Bake until the bread crumbs are browned and crisp and the cauliflower is bubbling, 25 to 35 minutes. Let cool for 5 to 10 minutes before serving.

MAC 'N' CHEEZE

My introduction, like many, to mac 'n' cheese was the blue box with the neon orange cheese powder. While the OG stuff is pretty darn good, a good homemade take, especially when tasted for the first time, is pretty revelatory. My own recipe starts with a thick, creamy béchamel to which tangy extra-sharp Cheddar, buttery fontina, and nutty Gruyère are added. As for the Ritz Crackers, they add a buttery, salty crunch that enhances, rather than overpowers, the sauce's flavors. It's all spectacularly rich and decadent, but totally worth each and every bite. This recipe can easily be halved for a smaller crowd.

Serves 4 to 6

1 Preheat the oven to 375°F. Butter or oil a 9 by 13 in [23 by 33 cm] baking dish.

2 In a small microwave-safe bowl, heat 1 Tbsp of the butter for 10 to 15 seconds, until fully melted. Add the Ritz Crackers and mix together. Set aside.

3 Bring a large pot of water to a boil and salt generously. Add the macaroni and cook for 1 minute less than the time specified on the package for al dente pasta. Drain well and let cool while you make the sauce.

4 In a large pot, melt the remaining 6 Tbsp [85 g] butter over medium heat. Add the flour all at once and quickly whisk into a paste. Continue to cook, stirring constantly, until the mixture smells biscuity and turns golden blond, about 2 minutes—don't let it brown too much. Gradually pour in the milk, a bit at a time, whisking constantly and thoroughly after each addition. Make sure you get into all corners of the pan to ensure a smooth, lump-free texture. The paste will initially become thick and then turn thin once all the milk has been added.

5 Bring to a boil. Continue to cook, stirring constantly, for 3 to 4 minutes, until the sauce thickens. Remove from the heat and wait until the sauce stops vigorously simmering before adding the Cheddar, fontina,

7 Tbsp [100 g] unsalted butter

1 cup [85 g] crushed Ritz Crackers

1 lb [455 g] elbow macaroni, small shells, or other short pasta

6 Tbsp [55 g] all-purpose flour

4 cups [960 ml] whole milk, warmed until hot but not boiling

8 oz [230 g] extra-sharp Cheddar cheese, coarsely grated (2 cups)

8 oz [230 g] fontina, coarsely grated (2 cups)

6 oz [170 g] Gruyère (or more fontina), coarsely grated (1½ cups)

1 Tbsp English dry mustard

1 Tbsp kosher salt

Hot sauce, such as Cholula or Tapatio, as needed

1 cup (4 oz [115 g]) of the Gruyère, the dry mustard, salt, and a few (or more) dashes of hot sauce.

6 Add the cooked macaroni and stir to evenly coat. Pour into the prepared baking dish. Sprinkle the remaining ½ cup (2 oz [55 g]) Gruyère over the top, followed by the crackers. Bake for 15 minutes, or until the cheese on top melts and the sauce begins to bubble around the edges. Let sit for 5 to 10 minutes before serving.

OAXACAN FOUR-ONION
QUESADILLAS
WITH JALAPEÑO AND LIME-PICKLED RED ONIONS

Yellow, red, and green onions, leeks, shallots, chives, and garlic . . . these are some of my favorite things. When kept raw and paired with melty cheese, as in this recipe, their sulfuric bite can cut through dairy's fat and coax out the inherent funk of a certain wedge. The lime-pickled red onions are just the right level of acidity to round out each bite with a pleasant sweetness.

Mexican Oaxaca is a semifirm cheese with a string-like texture that melts gorgeously, while Cotija is an aged crumbly wheel that provides a nice salty bite to the filling. Seek out both in a well-stocked grocery store or your local Latin grocery.

Makes 4 quesadillas

1 **To make the pickled onions:** In a small bowl, toss the red onions with the lime juice and season with salt. Set aside, tossing occasionally.

2 **To make the filling:** In a medium bowl, mix the Oaxaca and Cotija cheeses with the chives, leeks, chopped red onion, green onions, cilantro, garlic, and jalapeño.

3 Divide the filling evenly between the tortillas, spreading it on only half and leaving a ½ in [1.25 cm] border. Fold the tortillas over and seal the edges by pressing down firmly.

4 Place a baking sheet in the oven and preheat it to 300°F [150°C]. Line a plate with paper towels.

5 Add enough oil to coat the bottom of a large skillet (preferably 10 in [25 cm]) and heat over medium heat until shimmering. Carefully add 2 tortillas (or if your skillet is smaller, add just 1) and cook until the bottom is golden and crispy, about 2 minutes. Using a spatula, gently flip and cook until the second side is golden and crispy and the cheese has melted, another 2 minutes.

6 Transfer to the lined plate to drain. Then transfer the quesadillas to the baking sheet to keep warm while you repeat the process with the remaining tortillas.

7 When finished cooking, cut the quesadillas into triangles and serve immediately with sour cream and the lime-pickled red onions.

LIME-PICKLED RED ONIONS

½ red onion, cut into thin slices

2 Tbsp fresh lime juice

Kosher salt

—

FILLING

8 oz [230 g] Oaxaca cheese, Monterey Jack cheese, or low-moisture mozzarella cheese, coarsely grated (about 2 cups)

1 oz [30 g] Cotija, crumbled, or fresh Parmesan cheese, medium grated (⅓ cup)

¼ cup [15 g] minced chives

¼ cup [30 g] thinly sliced leek (see Note, page 118) or finely chopped shallots

¼ cup [35 g] finely chopped red onion

¼ cup [12 g] thinly sliced green onions

¼ cup [10 g] finely chopped fresh cilantro

2 garlic cloves, minced

½ to 1 jalapeño pepper, seeded and finely minced

—

Four 8 in [20 cm] flour tortillas

Vegetable or grapeseed oil, for frying

Sour cream, for serving

BAKED EGGS

IN SPICY TOMATO SAUCE
WITH TALEGGIO

Somewhere between a Middle Eastern shakshuka and Italian eggs in purgatory, these baked eggs are nestled into a jammy tomato, onion, and bell pepper sauce that's on the spicy side. Tying it all together with a hint of decadence is creamy and funky Taleggio. Served with hearty bread to mop up runny yolks, it's an any-time-of-day, one-pan meal that I never grow tired of.

You may be tempted to remove the rind from the Taleggio, but resist—it's packed with flavor! If you can't find Taleggio, then Brie, Camembert, or fresh mozzarella would work well as substitutes.

Serves 4 to 6

3 Tbsp extra-virgin olive oil

1 medium yellow onion, chopped

1 red bell pepper, stemmed, seeded, and chopped

Kosher salt

3 or 4 garlic cloves, cut into thin slices

1 tsp red pepper flakes, plus more if desired

One 28 oz [800 g] can diced tomatoes (preferably San Marzano)

1 Tbsp finely chopped parsley, plus more for garnish

¼ cup [10 g] roughly chopped basil, plus more for garnish

1 tsp sugar or honey, plus more if desired (optional)

3 to 4 oz [85 to 115 g] cold Taleggio cheese

4 to 6 eggs

Freshly ground black pepper

Crusty bread, for serving

1 Preheat the oven to 375°F [190°C].

2 In a 12 in [30.5 cm] ovenproof skillet, heat the oil over medium heat. Add the onion, bell pepper, and a big pinch of salt and cook until the vegetables soften and the onion begins to turn translucent.

3 Add the garlic and red pepper flakes and cook for 1 minute more. Stir in the diced tomatoes, parsley, basil, and another big pinch of salt. Bring to a simmer over medium-high heat, turn the heat to medium, and simmer for 12 to 15 minutes, or until the sauce thickens and becomes jam-like. Season with salt and sugar to offset the sauce's acidity, if needed. Turn the heat to low.

4 Meanwhile, cut the Taleggio into slices and then cut the slices into roughly 1 in [2.5 cm] pieces. When the sauce is done cooking, evenly nestle the Taleggio pieces into the sauce. With the back of a large spoon, create an indent in the sauce and gently crack an egg into it. Repeat with the remaining eggs. Season the eggs with salt and black pepper. Transfer to the oven and bake until the whites set, 6 to 10 minutes.

5 Garnish with more parsley and basil and serve immediately with hearty, crusty bread. Any leftovers can be refrigerated for up to 1 day.

SMOKED GOUDA

CHICKEN CORDON BLEU

I remember my family going through a chicken cordon bleu phase when I was a kid—the kind you'd buy in a blue box and bake up from frozen. They were like over-size chicken nuggets that oozed cheese, so go figure I loved them so much. This homemade version is a bit more refined but is just as satisfying to eat. For a bit more oomph, I replace Swiss with smoked Gouda and add whole grain mustard, and to achieve that perfect log shape, I borrow a technique from Tyler Florence. Toasting the bread crumbs gives the rolls a beauti-ful brown exterior, but if you're OK with a light shell, you can skip it.

Feel free to substitute the smoked Gouda with regular Gouda or another melty semifirm cheese like Gruyère, Raclette, Cheddar, or fontina. Experiment with other baked styles of ham or go the cured route with prosciutto, Serrano ham, or speck.

Serves 4

1 Preheat the oven to 400°F [200°C].

2 Combine the bread crumbs and parsley on a baking sheet. Season with salt and pepper and drizzle with the melted butter. Toss until the bread crumbs are fully saturated with butter and then spread in an even layer. Bake until lightly golden, 3 to 4 minutes. Transfer to a shallow bowl and set aside.

3 Lower the heat to 350°F [180°C] and line the same baking sheet with parchment paper. Have the ingredients for seasoning and filling the chicken measured into bowls or set out and within easy reach to streamline the process. Have a large plate ready nearby.

1 cup [60 g] panko bread crumbs

2 Tbsp finely chopped flat-leaf parsley

Kosher salt

Freshly ground black pepper

2 Tbsp unsalted butter, melted

4 boneless and skinless chicken breasts

4 Tbsp [60 g] whole grain mustard

4 slices Black Forest ham

8 oz [230 g] smoked Gouda, coarsely grated (about 2 cups)

¼ cup [35 g] all-purpose flour

1 egg

Salad, roasted vegetables, or Cheddar Sour Cream and Onion Hasselback Potato Gratin (page 130), for serving

4 Use the flat side of a meat mallet to flatten 1 of the chicken breasts between two pieces of plastic wrap until ¼ in [6 mm] thick. Remove the top sheet of plastic. Season with salt and pepper and smear evenly with 1 Tbsp of the mustard. Place 1 ham slice over the top to cover the breast and top with one-quarter of the cheese. Tuck the edges in if needed and roll up the chicken breast into a tight pinwheel. Tightly wrap up the chicken roll in plastic wrap and twist both ends tight, as if you're wrapping a candy, to create a log. Transfer to the plate. Repeat the process with the remaining chicken and refrigerate for 10 to 15 minutes.

5 Meanwhile put the flour in a shallow bowl and lightly beat the egg in another shallow bowl. Season both with salt and pepper. Remove the plastic wrap from the chicken rolls. Working with 1 roll at a time, dredge the chicken in the flour, shaking off the excess. Gently dip into the egg and then evenly coat with the prepared panko, pressing gently to adhere. Transfer to the prepared baking sheet, seam-side down.

6 Depending on the size of your chicken breast, bake for 30 to 40 minutes, or until cooked through and a digital thermometer reads 160 to 165°F [70 to 75°C]. Let sit for 5 to 10 minutes before serving with salad or roasted vegetables, or the Cheddar, Sour Cream, and Onion Hasselback Potato Gratin (page 130) for an extra-cheesy meal.

RUSSIAN

FRENCH-STYLE

CHICKEN

I grew up with my mom making this sheet pan dish anytime we had guests. I never questioned the name (a Google search will tell you about a Count Orloff and his French chef) because I was too busy devouring it. This is her recipe, slightly adapted, and it couldn't be easier—simply layer chicken with onions, bell peppers, Swiss cheese, and mayonnaise. The mayo keeps the chicken tender and moist, and the cheese turns melty and golden. My favorite part, however, are the peppers and onions—they cook just long enough to sweeten and lose their raw edge without sacrificing their bite.

Serves 4 to 6

1 Preheat the oven to 350°F [180°C].

2 Season both sides of chicken thighs with salt and pepper and then transfer the chicken to a 9 by 13 in [23 by 33 cm] baking dish to make an even base layer. Top with an even layer of the onion, bell pepper, and cheese. Sprinkle all over with the lemon juice. Using an offset spatula or the back of a spoon, carefully top the cheese with an even layer of mayonnaise (you're basically pressing it into the Swiss to make a mayo-cheese layer)—try not to move around the peppers and onions too much. Season with salt and the cayenne. The chicken dish can be made up to 2 days in advance, wrapped in plastic wrap, and refrigerated.

3 Bake for 40 to 45 minutes, or until the chicken is cooked through and the cheese is browned on top. Let sit for 10 minutes before serving. Serve with rice or mashed potatoes on the side.

2 lb [910 g] boneless and skinless chicken thighs, excess fat trimmed

Kosher salt

Freshly ground black pepper

1 small onion, cut into thin slices

½ green bell pepper, stemmed, seeded, and cut into ¼ in [6 mm] slices

½ orange or red bell pepper, stemmed, seeded, and cut into ¼ in [6 mm] slices

8 oz [230 g] Swiss or baby Swiss cheese, coarsely grated (about 2 cups)

2 Tbsp fresh lemon juice

⅔ cup [160 g] mayonnaise

1 tsp cayenne pepper

Rice or mashed potatoes, for serving

STUFFED PORK

TENDERLOIN WITH SHALLOTS, APPLE, AND FONTINA

2 Tbsp unsalted butter

2 large shallots, chopped

1 large Granny Smith apple, peeled, cored, and cut into ½ in [12 mm] dice

Kosher salt

3 garlic cloves, minced

2 tsp minced fresh rosemary

Freshly ground black pepper

1½ lb [680 g] pork tenderloin, silver skin trimmed

4 oz [115 g] fontina, coarsely grated (1 cup)

Extra-virgin olive oil, for brushing

While this juicy pork tenderloin—stuffed with rosemary-flecked apples, shallots, and a melty layer of fontina cheese—may look fancy and complicated, broken down, the recipe is quite doable. Once you know the technique, you'll be able to take this inexpensive cut and fill it with whatever inspires you for an impressive main dish. Pork tenderloin usually comes in packs of two, so you can easily double this recipe as a no-fuss way to feed a crowd. It's perfect paired with hearty greens—sautéed or massaged into a salad—or even rice.

Feel free to substitute any semifirm cheese, such as provolone, Gruyère, or Gouda, for the fontina.

Serves 4

1 Melt the butter in a large skillet over medium-high heat. Add the shallots and cook until they begin to soften, about 2 minutes. Add the apple and a big pinch of salt and cook, stirring often, until the shallots and apple begin to brown and caramelize, about 5 minutes. Lower the heat to medium, add the garlic and rosemary, and cook for 1 minute more. Remove from the heat and season with salt and pepper. Let cool completely before assembling the pork. This filling can be stored in an airtight container and refrigerated for up to 3 days.

2 Preheat the oven to 450°F [230°C]. Line a baking sheet with aluminum foil and butter or oil it.

3 Put the pork on a large cutting board with the short side facing you. With a sharp chef's knife parallel to the board, ½ in [12 mm] from the bottom of the tenderloin, make a lengthwise cut toward the center, stopping within ½ in [12 mm] of the other side. Open up the tenderloin and continue to make shallow cuts along the same line, using your other hand to open up and unroll the pork while doing so. The pork will eventually lay open and will form a pinwheel when you roll it back up.

4 Cover the pork with plastic wrap and pound it with a meat mallet to flatten it into an even ¼ to ½ in [6 to 12 mm] thickness. Remove the plastic wrap and season generously with salt and pepper.

5 Spread the filling evenly over the surface of the pork, leaving 1 in [2.5 cm] around the edges so you can roll it up. Sprinkle the fontina over the filling in an even layer. Starting with the long side closest to you, tightly roll up the tenderloin.

6 Tie the tenderloin together with eight 12 in [30.5 cm] pieces of kitchen twine at about 1½ in [4 cm] intervals. Season the outside of the pork generously with salt and pepper and brush evenly with olive oil. The tenderloin can be kept covered and refrigerated for up to 2 days. Bring to room temperature before continuing, about 30 minutes.

7 Place on the baking sheet and roast for 25 minutes, or until a digital thermometer reads 140°F [60°C] in the thickest part of the meat (the pork will continue to cook after it is removed from the oven). Let the tenderloin rest for 10 to 15 minutes. Transfer to a cutting board, remove the twine, and cut into slices before serving.

SHEPHERD'S PIE

TATER TOT

HOT DISH

Hailing from the upper Midwest, this hot dish is the sort of stick-to-your ribs comfort food that will warm you right up, no matter how cold it is outside. The hodge-podge one-dish meal is comprised of meat, canned vegetables, and condensed cream soup and is topped with anything from fried onions to potato chips to La Choy chow mein noodles. It may look a bit dubious, but it'll quickly win you over once you start digging in. This particular version is reminiscent of shepherd's pie but with crispy, browned tater tots and melty Cheddar cheese rather than mashed potatoes to top it all off. Next time snow is in the forecast, pick up some tots and you'll be ready to go!

Serves 4 to 6

1 Preheat the oven to 350°F. Butter or oil a 9 by 13 in [23 by 33 cm] baking dish.

2 In a large saucepan or pot, melt 6 Tbsp [85 g] of the butter over medium heat. Add half of the onion, the carrot, celery, and a pinch of salt and cook until the vegetables soften and the onion turns translucent, 7 to 8 minutes. Add the garlic and cook for 1 minute more. Add the flour and stir to incorporate it into the vegetables—they will clump into one dry mass. Cook for 2 minutes. Slowly begin to stir in the milk a little bit at a time, waiting until the vegetable-flour mixture absorbs the liquid before pouring in more. Stir in the chicken bouillon base. Bring to a simmer and cook, stirring frequently, for 2 to 3 minutes, or until the sauce has thickened and coats the back of a spoon. Remove from the heat and set aside.

3 In a large skillet, melt the remaining 1 Tbsp butter over medium heat. Add the remaining onion and a pinch of salt and cook for 3 to 4 minutes

-cont.

7 Tbsp [100 g] unsalted butter

1 medium yellow onion, diced

1 medium carrot, peeled and diced

1 celery stalk, diced

Kosher salt

2 garlic cloves, minced

6 Tbsp [55 g] all-purpose flour

2 cups [480 ml] whole milk

2 tsp chicken or beef bouillon base, or 1 bouillon cube

1 lb [455 g] 80 or 85% ground beef

2 cups [240 to 280 g] frozen corn, peas, or a combination of the two

1 Tbsp Worcestershire sauce

⅓ cup [80 g] sour cream

One 2 lb [910 g] bag frozen tater tots

8 oz [230 g] sharp Cheddar cheese, coarsely grated (2 cups)

to soften. Increase the heat to medium-high, add the beef, and cook until browned, another 3 to 4 minutes. Stir in the corn (and/or peas, if using) and cook for 1 minute more to warm through. Remove from the heat and season with the Worcestershire sauce and salt. Add the beef-corn mixture to the pan with the creamed soup base. Add the sour cream and mix to combine. Transfer the mixture to the prepared baking dish. Cooled and covered, the hot dish can be refrigerated for up to 2 days in advance.

4 Top with even rows of tater tots (feel free to play around with the design) and bake for 50 minutes, or until the tater tots are browned and crispy. Remove from the oven, sprinkle with the cheese, and continue baking until the cheese melts, another 10 minutes. Let cool for 5 to 10 minutes before serving.

HELLGIRL PIZZA

This dish is inspired by one of my favorite restaurants—Lampo Neopolitan Pizzeria in Charlottesville, Virginia. They have a 9,000 lb [4,000 kg] wood-fire oven imported from Italy and it churns out the most beautifully flame-licked Neapolitan-style 'zas. Their Hellboy in particular, with its crisped hot salami, sizzling pools of mozzarella, and spicy scorpion chile honey, has garnered a cult following. Born out of my own cravings, the Hellgirl is my take on that mouthwatering round—a little taste of Charlottesville. You can also substitute a drizzle of regular honey and red pepper flakes for the hot honey.

Makes 2 pizzas

1 Remove the dough from the refrigerator. Divide into two equal pieces, shape into rounds, and transfer to a well-floured large plate or small baking sheet with plenty of room between them. Dust with more flour and lightly cover with plastic wrap or a clean kitchen towel. Let the dough sit unit it comes to room temperature, 60 to 90 minutes.

2 Position a rack in the upper third of the oven. Turn the broiler on high and preheat for 30 minutes.

3 Meanwhile, in a food processor or blender, pulse the tomatoes with their juices until chunky, about 6 seconds. Alternatively, transfer the tomatoes and their juices to a medium bowl and crush by hand. Season with salt and set aside. Have the rest of your toppings ready to go.

4 When ready to bake, heat a 10 to 12 in [25 to 30.5 cm] cast-iron or ovenproof skillet over medium-high heat for 3 to 5 minutes. Meanwhile, transfer one dough round to a well-floured surface, keeping the other covered. Lightly dust with flour and gently work the dough, pressing from the inside out and stretching, into a 10 to 12 in [25 to 30.5 cm] round. Dust with more flour if the dough starts to become sticky at any point.

5 Carefully transfer to the hot skillet, using your fingers or shaking the skillet to carefully arrange it into place.

—cont.

1 lb [445 g] homemade or store-bought pizza dough

14½ oz [415 g] can whole peeled tomatoes

Kosher salt

8 oz [230 g] fresh mozzarella cheese, sliced

2 oz [55 g] hot soppressata

2 oz [55 g] fresh Parmesan cheese, coarsely grated (½ cup), plus more for garnish

Hot Honey (recipe follows) or store-bought honey, for drizzling

Fresh basil leaves, for garnish

6 Working quickly, add a thin layer of tomato sauce (about ¼ cup [60 ml]), leaving a ¾ to 1 in [2 to 2.5 cm] border. Top with half of the mozzarella, 6 or 7 slices of the soppressata, and half the Parmesan. Continue to cook on medium-high heat until the bottom starts to develop brown spots all around (use a spatula to lift up the edges to check), 1 to 4 minutes.

7 Carefully transfer the skillet to the oven and broil, rotating the pan halfway through to ensure even cooking, until the edges are puffed and lightly charred and the bottom is crisp, 3 to 6 minutes. Remove from the oven and transfer to a cutting board. Garnish with more Parmesan, a drizzle of hot honey, and fresh basil. Slice and serve immediately. Meanwhile, turn the broiler back on and repeat the process to make a second pizza.

HOT HONEY

Honey infused with hot pepper couldn't be easier. Save your expensive raw honey for another time; use pasteurized (the kind sold in plastic bears) instead to prevent crystallization. For a less spicy honey, remove the seeds. Fresno chiles are often labeled red jalapeños at the grocery store. To save yourself from any unnecessary pain, use gloves when handling the peppers.

Makes 1 cup [340 g] honey

1 Add the honey and fresh and dried peppers to a small saucepan. Bring to a boil over medium heat. Turn the heat to low and simmer until the honey is infused with chile flavor and spice, about 10 minutes. Strain the honey through a fine-mesh sieve over a bowl and transfer to an airtight glass jar or storage container. Let cool completely before storing and using. The honey will keep for 2 weeks at room temperature and for 1 month refrigerated.

1 cup [340 g] light honey, such as clover

2 Fresno or other medium-hot red peppers, stemmed, halved, and cut into thin slices

1 dried red chile (such as Thai, Fresno, or chile de árbol), crushed

CHORIZO,
SWEET POTATO, AND KALE
ENCHILADAS

Don't let the preparation of these enchiladas scare you. Make the sauce and filling ahead of time, and when it comes time to assemble, all you'll have to do is fry and fill the tortillas and smother them in sauce and cheese before baking. You may be tempted to skip pre-cooking the tortillas, but don't—not only does it bring out their flavor and soften them for rolling, but also prevents them from turning soggy. If you can't find 6 in [15 cm] corn tortillas, use the smaller 4 in [10 cm] and fill them with a bit less filling—you will get about 14 to 16 stuffed enchiladas that way.

To make this dish vegetarian, substitute black beans for the chorizo and cook them with the shallots until they're warmed.

Serves 4 to 6

1 **To make the enchilada sauce:** Heat the oil in a small saucepan over medium heat. Whisk in the flour and cook for 1 minute, until pale brown. Add the chili powder, cumin, oregano, garlic powder,

onion powder, sugar, and cinnamon and cook for another 30 seconds to bloom the spices. Gradually stir in the chicken stock a little bit at a time, waiting until the mixture absorbs the liquid before pouring in more. Stir in the tomato sauce and chipotle pepper purée. Bring to a simmer and cook for 8 to 10 minutes, until the sauce has thickened and has lost its acidic tang. Remove from the heat, season with salt, and set aside. The sauce can be covered and refrigerated for up to 5 days.

2 **To make the filling:** In a large skillet, heat the oil over medium heat. Add the onion and a pinch of salt and cook until the onion softens and begins to turn translucent, about 5 minutes. Add the garlic and cook for 1 minute more. Add the chorizo, breaking up large chunks with your spoon, and cook until browned and cooked through, 5 to 6 minutes. Season with salt. Use a slotted spoon to transfer the chorizo mixture to a medium bowl. Reserve the fat in the skillet.

-cont.

ENCHILADA SAUCE

2 Tbsp neutral oil, such as canola

2 Tbsp all-purpose flour

1½ Tbsp chili powder

1½ tsp ground cumin

1 tsp dried oregano

½ tsp garlic powder

½ tsp onion powder

½ tsp sugar

⅛ tsp ground cinnamon

1½ cups [360 ml] chicken or vegetable stock

One 8 oz [230 g] can tomato sauce

1½ Tbsp Chipotle Pepper Purée (page 64)

Kosher salt

—

FILLING

1 Tbsp neutral oil, such as canola

1 small yellow onion, chopped

Kosher salt

2 cloves garlic, cut into thin slices

12 oz [340 g] chorizo (casings removed if necessary)

1 large sweet potato (about 1 lb [455 g]), cut into ½ in [12 mm] dice

1 tsp ground cumin

½ tsp ground coriander

1 small bunch dinosaur kale (about 8 oz [230 g]), stemmed and roughly chopped

4 oz [115 g] shredded Mexican cheese blend (1 cup)

—

Neutral oil, such as canola, for frying

Twelve 6 in [15 cm] yellow corn tortillas

8 oz [230 g] shredded Mexican cheese blend (2 cups)

Fresh cilantro leaves, roughly chopped, for garnish

Sour cream, for serving

3 Heat the reserved fat in the skillet over medium heat. Add the sweet potato, cumin, coriander, and a big pinch of salt and toss to coat completely in the reserved fat. Cook, stirring occasionally, until cooked through, 15 to 20 minutes. Add the kale one large handful at a time, allowing the first batch to wilt before adding more, and cook until tender, another 2 to 3 minutes. Season with salt and transfer to the bowl with the chorizo. Stir the mixture together and allow to slightly cool before adding the cheese. Season with salt if necessary and set aside. The filling can be made up to 4 days in advance.

4 Preheat the oven to 350°F. Spread one-fourth of the enchilada sauce in the bottom of a 9 by 13 [23 by 33 cm] baking dish. Line a large plate with paper towels.

5 In a small or medium skillet, add enough oil to coat the bottom of the pan and heat over medium heat. When the oil is shimmering and hot, using tongs, add a tortilla to the pan. Cook for 8 to 10 seconds (the tortilla will begin to bubble) before flipping and cooking for another 10 seconds— you just want to soften the tortillas, so make sure you're not browning them. Transfer to the paper towel– lined plate. Repeat with the remaining tortillas.

6 Lay a tortilla on a plate and place about ⅓ cup [55 g] of the chorizo- sweet potato filling in the center. Roll into a cylinder and place seam-side down in the prepared baking dish. Repeat with the remaining tortillas, nestling the filled tortillas tightly in the dish. Pour the rest of the sauce over the tortillas to evenly cover, and sprinkle with the cheese. Bake until the cheese has melted and the sauce begins to bubble, 20 to 25 minutes. Garnish with cilantro and serve with sour cream.

BUTTERNUT SQUASH, RICOTTA, AND PANCETTA

STUFFED SHELLS

WITH BAKED BURRATA

Who knew that, when torn over your pasta and baked, Burrata—essentially mozzarella stuffed with curds and cream—can transform into an effortless melty and gooey sauce? Here, the cheese blankets pasta shells stuffed with roasted butternut squash, pillowy ricotta, and crispy pancetta for a wintertime dish that is as comforting as it is satisfying. Make this vegetarian by omitting the pancetta.

Serves 4

1 Preheat the oven to 400°F [200°C]. Line a plate with paper towels.

2 On a large baking sheet, toss the squash with the oil and season with 1 tsp of salt. Spread evenly on the sheet. Bake for 25 to 30 minutes, or until fork tender and lightly browned. Let cool.

3 Meanwhile, bring a large pot of water to a boil over high heat and salt generously. Add the pasta shells and cook according to the package directions until al dente. Drain and let cool completely. Set aside.

4 In a large skillet, cook the pancetta over medium heat until the fat renders and the pancetta is golden and crispy, 6 to 8 minutes. With a slotted spoon, transfer the pancetta to the prepared plate. Discard all but 1 Tbsp of the fat.

5 Add the red onion and a pinch of salt to the same skillet and cook over medium heat, stirring frequently, until the onion begins to soften, about 5 minutes. Add the garlic and cook for 1 minute more. Add the wine and deglaze the pan, stirring to scrape up the browned bits from the bottom of the skillet. Cook until the liquid evaporates, about 2 minutes. Remove from the heat and set aside.

-cont.

1 lb [455 g] butternut squash, cut into ½ in [6.5 cm] cubes (3 cups)

2 tsp olive oil

Kosher salt

20 jumbo pasta shells

3 thick slices pancetta, diced (about 6 oz [170 g])

½ medium red onion, chopped

2 garlic cloves, cut into thin slices

2 Tbsp dry white wine

13 oz [370 g] ricotta cheese (about 1½ cups)

¼ cup [60 ml] heavy cream

1 Tbsp minced fresh sage

1½ oz [40 g] fresh Parmesan cheese, medium grated (about ½ cup)

2 tsp lemon zest

Freshly cracked black pepper

8 oz [230 g] Burrata cheese

6 In a medium bowl, mix the ricotta with the heavy cream, sage, half of the Parmesan, and lemon zest. Fold in the pancetta, red onion, and butternut squash. Season with salt and black pepper.

7 Butter an 8 by 11 in [20 by 28 cm] baking dish. Stuff each pasta shell with the filling and snuggle the shells into the baking dish. The assembled dish can be wrapped in plastic wrap and refrigerated for up to 2 days.

8 Cover the dish with aluminum foil and bake for 20 minutes, until cooked through. Remove from the oven and remove the foil. Tear the Burrata into pieces over the dish, allowing its creamy interior to spread evenly over and around the pasta. Sprinkle with the remaining Parmesan and season with black pepper. Return to the oven and cook until the cheese is melted, about 10 minutes. Serve immediately.

PENNE ALLA VODKA

WITH SAUSAGE AND SMOKED MOZZARELLA

My mom used to throw a big handful of shredded mozzarella into a pot of plain, buttered pasta, tossing it around until the cheese stuck and stretched as she pulled the spoon away. It was a simple trick that left our dinner feeling extra comforting that night. The idea is the same here except that I've added a meaty vodka sauce with a bit of a kick and smoked mozzarella for depth of flavor. Cooked all in one pan (besides the pot for boiling pasta) on the stovetop, this hearty pasta dish will satisfy with its gooey cheese pulls for days.

Serves 4 to 6

1 In a deep, straight-sided sauté pan or Dutch oven, heat the oil and butter over medium heat. Add the onion, garlic, and a big pinch of salt and cook, stirring frequently, until the onion begins to soften, about 5 minutes. Add the sausage and red pepper flakes and cook, mashing with your spoon or spatula to break up the pieces, until the sausage is no longer pink, 4 to 5 minutes. Pour in the vodka and deglaze the pan, stirring to scrape up the browned bits from the bottom of the pot. Stir in the crushed tomatoes, oregano, basil, bay leaf, and a big pinch of salt. Bring to a boil over medium-high heat and then lower the heat to a simmer and cook for 30 minutes uncovered, until the sauce thickens.

2 Meanwhile, bring a large pot of generously salted water to a boil. Add the penne and cook according to the package directions until just al dente. Reserve 1 cup [240 ml] of the pasta water before draining.

3 When the sauce is done, remove the bay leaf and herb sprigs. Stir in the cream and a ladle of the pasta water. Increase the heat to medium, add the pasta to the pan, and toss to

2 Tbsp extra-virgin olive oil

1 Tbsp unsalted butter

1 medium yellow onion, finely diced

3 or 4 garlic cloves, cut into thin slices

Kosher salt

1 lb [455 g] hot or sweet Italian sausage, casings removed

½ tsp red pepper flakes, plus more if desired

½ cup [120 ml] vodka

One 28 oz [800 g] can crushed tomatoes (preferably San Marzano)

2 fresh oregano sprigs

1 large or 2 small fresh basil sprigs

1 fresh or dried bay leaf

1 lb [455 g] dry penne or ziti pasta

½ cup [120 ml] heavy cream

6 oz [170 g] low-moisture whole milk mozzarella cheese, coarsely grated (1½ cups)

4 oz [115 g] smoked mozzarella cheese, coarsely grated (1 cup)

3 oz [85 g] fresh Parmesan cheese, medium grated (1 cup), plus more for sprinkling

coat. Continue cooking, adding pasta water as needed and stirring frequently, until the pasta is coated in a rich and silky sauce and is perfectly al dente, 3 to 5 minutes.

4 Stir in three-fourths of both mozzarellas and all of the Parmesan cheese until evenly distributed and melted— although don't stir too much, or the cheese will stick to your spoon. Sprinkle the pasta with the remaining mozzarellas. Cover, remove from the heat, and let sit for at least 5 to 8 minutes to melt the cheese on top. Uncover, sprinkle with Parmesan, and serve immediately.

SUPPORTING
SIDES

~~~

CELERIAC, POTATO, AND APPLE ROSEMARY

GRATIN WITH COMTÉ

Knobby, alien-like celeriac—or celery root—is an underrated and overlooked root vegetable in my book. Its flavor is earthier and nuttier than regular celery and its crunchy, sturdy texture lends itself to both raw and cooked applications. For this recipe, celeriac takes center stage, along with creamy potatoes and tart apples, coated in a leek and rosemary–flecked béchamel sauce and sweet and brown-buttery Comté cheese before baking. The result is a deeply satisfying and aromatic gratin that hits all the right notes without feeling too heavy.

Serve it alongside roasted chicken or panfried pork chops—or better yet, with a simple mustardy salad on the side for a comforting vegetarian main.

Note: To properly clean leeks, remove the dark green parts that are tough.

Without cutting through the end, make a slice lengthwise. Rotate and make another lengthwise cut. Run under cold water, making sure you remove any sediment between the layers. Pat dry before continuing.

Serves 4 to 6

1 Fill a large pot halfway with water. Place over high heat, bring to a boil, and generously salt the water. Once it's boiling again, cook the celeriac and potato, adding more water if needed to cover the vegetables by at least 1 in [2.5 cm], for 5 to 6 minutes, or until a knife slides into them fairly easily but meets some resistance in the center.

2 Drain the vegetables thoroughly and set them aside to cool and release their steam while making the béchamel.

1 medium celeriac (about 1 lb [455 g]), peeled and cut into ¼ in [6 mm] thick slices

1 large russet potato (about 1 lb [455 g]), peeled and cut into ¼ in [6 mm] thick slices

3 Tbsp [45 g] unsalted butter

1 large leek, washed thoroughly (see Note), dark green top removed, quartered lengthwise, and cut into thin slices crosswise

Kosher salt

2 garlic cloves, cut into thin slices

2½ tsp minced fresh rosemary (about 1 large sprig)

3 Tbsp all-purpose flour

2 cups [480 ml] half-and-half or whole milk

8 oz [230 g] Comté or Gruyère, coarsely grated (2 cups)

1 Tbsp plus 1 tsp Dijon mustard

1 large tart apple, preferably Granny Smith, peeled, cored, and cut into ¼ in [6 mm] thick slices

Freshly ground black pepper

3 Preheat the oven to 350° F [180°C].

4 In a large pot over medium-low heat, melt the butter. Add the leek and a big pinch of salt and cook, stirring often, for 5 to 6 minutes, or until the leek begins to soften. Stir in the garlic and 2 tsp of the rosemary and cook for another 2 to 3 minutes.

5 Add the flour and stir to incorporate it into the leek—they will clump into one dry mass—and cook for 2 to 3 minutes. Slowly begin to stir in the half-and-half a little bit at a time, waiting until the leek-flour mixture absorbs the liquid before pouring in more. Bring to a slight simmer and cook, stirring frequently to keep the bottom from burning, for 2 to 3 minutes, or until the sauce has thickened and coats the back of a spoon.

6 Turn the heat to low and stir in 1½ cups [170 g] of the Comté and the mustard. Season with salt. Once the cheese has melted, add the celeriac, potato, and apple and mix until fully coated. Transfer to a 7 by 11 in [17 by 28 cm] baking dish and spread the mixture out into one even layer.

7 Sprinkle with the remaining ½ cup [60 g] of Comté and the remaining ½ tsp rosemary, and season with a few cracks of black pepper.

8 Bake for 45 to 50 minutes, or until the top is golden brown, the sauce is bubbling, and the potatoes and celeriac are fork tender. Let cool slightly before serving. You can also make the gratin a few hours ahead and let it stand at room temperature. Before serving, cover it with foil and warm in the oven at 350°F [180°C] for 15 to 20 minutes, or until hot throughout.

TWICE-BAKED
SWEET POTATOES

WITH RAS EL HANOUT CHICKPEAS AND CHÈVRE

3 medium (10 to 12 oz [285 to 340 g]) sweet potatoes

One 15½ oz [440 g] can chickpeas, well drained

2 garlic cloves, cut into thin slices

2 Tbsp olive oil

1½ tsp ras el hanout, plus more if desired

Kosher salt

6 oz [170 g] chèvre

1 Tbsp whole milk

Fresh mint leaves, for garnish

Roasted pepitas, for garnish

Flaky sea salt, for garnish

I have a bit of an addiction to sweet potatoes—I eat them at least two or three times a week. To keep from falling into the same ol' plain roasted route, I came up with this twice-baked take. Little "canoes" cradle creamy sweet potato filling that's studded with crispy chickpeas and flavored with tangy fresh chèvre and ras el hanout—a savory North African spice blend that's vibrant, earthy, and warm from spices like cinnamon, cardamom, turmeric, and ginger. Crunchy pepitas and bright mint tie this fun and satisfying yet healthy side together.

If you can't find ras el hanout, substitute an equal amount of curry powder or garam masala.

Serves 4 to 6

1 Preheat the oven to 400°F [200°C]. Line a baking sheet with parchment paper or aluminum foil.

2 Scrub and wash the sweet potatoes and poke all over with a fork to allow steam to escape. Put on the prepared baking sheet and bake for 55 to 60 minutes, or until fork tender. Let cool for at least 10 minutes.

3 Meanwhile, in a large skillet, toss the chickpeas with the garlic and olive oil. Cook over medium-high heat for 4 to 5 minutes, or until the chickpeas begin to turn a shade darker and crispy and some begin to split open. Remove from the heat and toss with the ras el hanout. Season with salt and set aside.

4 Preheat the oven again to 400°F [200°C].

5 Once the sweet potatoes are cool enough to handle, use a sharp knife to cut them in half lengthwise. Scoop out the flesh from each half, leaving a ¼ to ½ in [6 to 12 mm] rim of sweet potato intact for support—they will look like small canoes. Transfer the scooped flesh to a medium bowl. Add two-thirds of the chèvre and the milk and mix to combine. Mix in the chickpeas and season with salt and more ras el hanout, as desired.

6 Sprinkle each sweet potato half with salt and ras el hanout before stuffing them with the chèvre-chickpea filling. Return the stuffed sweet potatoes to the oven for 20 minutes, or until the filling begins to lightly brown on top.

7 Evenly distribute the remaining chèvre among the sweet potatoes and garnish with mint, pepitas, and flaky sea salt before serving.

ROASTED ASPARAGUS

WITH HERBED CHEESE SAUCE

Velvety smooth cheese sauce—packed with bright herbs and lemon—enrobes crispy roasted asparagus in this perfect springtime dish. Think hollandaise but without the headache and twice the flavor. Plus, hot cheese! And, it's lightning-quick to prepare: If you have all the ingredients ready to go, the sauce comes together in the time the asparagus roasts. Serve it with salmon for a weeknight dinner or at your next brunch on toast with poached eggs.

Serves 4

1 Preheat the oven to 425°F [220°C].

2 Assemble the asparagus in an even layer on a baking sheet (or divide between two if they don't all fit), drizzle with the olive oil, and season with a big pinch of salt and black pepper. Toss to coat. Cook for about 12 minutes, or until the asparagus is bright green and slightly tender.

3 **Meanwhile, to make the cheese sauce:** In a small bowl, mix the cornstarch and 1 Tbsp of the evaporated milk into a slurry. Pour the rest of the evaporated milk into a medium saucepan and stir in the slurry. Bring the milk to a boil over medium-high heat, whisking constantly. Turn the heat to low and add the mozzarella and Parmesan gradually by the handful, stirring until melted and the mixture is smooth. Stir in the garlic, basil, parsley, lemon juice, and zest. Season with salt, black pepper, and cayenne.

4 When the asparagus is done cooking, transfer it to a serving dish. Pour the herbed cheese sauce over the asparagus and serve. Any leftover sauce can be stored in an airtight container and refrigerated for up to 3 days—to reheat before serving, microwave the sauce, stirring every 30 seconds, until fully melted.

---

2 bunches asparagus, woody ends removed

2 tsp extra-virgin olive oil

Kosher salt

Freshly cracked black pepper

—

HERBED CHEESE SAUCE

1 Tbsp cornstarch

One 12 fl oz [360 ml] can evaporated milk

8 oz [230 g] low-moisture whole milk mozzarella, fontina, or provolone cheese, or a combination, coarsely grated (2 cups)

2 oz [55 g] fresh Parmesan cheese, coarsely grated (½ cup)

1 garlic clove, finely grated

2 Tbsp finely chopped fresh basil

2 Tbsp finely chopped fresh flat-leaf parsley

1 Tbsp fresh lemon juice

1 tsp lemon zest

Big pinch of cayenne pepper

CREAMED WINTER GREENS WITH GRUYÈRE

DROP BISCUITS

This dish is for the dead of the winter, when greens like kale, chard, spinach, and collards are at their prime and you're looking for something to warm you up from the inside out. The greens are coated in just enough nutmeg-spiced cream to keep them from getting soggy, while cheesy buttermilk drop biscuits—tender, fluffy, and quick to pull together—make every bite more texturally interesting and the end result impressive. As a bonus, they sop up any extra sauce. Serve this dish as part of a holiday spread or a hearty weekend meal.

You can substitute any good semifirm melting cheese for the Gruyère, such as fontina, Cheddar, Comté, or Gouda.

Serves 4

1 Preheat the oven to 400°F [200°C]. Prepare a large bowl with ice-cold water.

2 Bring a large pot of water to a boil and salt generously. Blanch the kale in the salted water for about 3 minutes, or until just softened, pushing the greens down periodically as needed to fully submerge them. Using a slotted spoon or skimmer, transfer the kale to the ice water to keep them from cooking further. Drain and, working in handfuls, squeeze out the excess water. Set the greens aside.

3 Bring the water back up to a boil and fill the bowl with ice water again. Blanch the Swiss chard for about 1 minute. Transfer to the ice water, drain, and squeeze out the excess water. Roughly chop both the kale and the chard and set aside.

4 Heat a large ovenproof sauté pan or skillet over medium heat. Add the butter and, once it has melted, add the garlic and thyme sprigs. Cook for about 1 minute, stirring

Kosher salt

1 lb [455 g] kale, stemmed (about 1 large bunch)

1 lb [455 g] Swiss chard, stemmed (about 2 small bunches)

2 Tbsp unsalted butter

4 garlic cloves, smashed

2 fresh thyme sprigs

1 large onion, chopped

3 Tbsp dry white wine, or 1½ Tbsp white wine vinegar

1 cup [240 ml] heavy cream

3 oz [85 g] Gruyère, coarsely grated (¾ cup)

¼ tsp ground nutmeg

¼ tsp cayenne pepper, plus more if desired

—

DROP BISCUITS

1 cup [140 g] all-purpose flour

1 tsp baking powder

1 tsp sugar

¾ tsp kosher salt

¼ tsp baking soda

⅛ tsp cayenne pepper

4 Tbsp cold unsalted butter, cubed

3 oz [85 g] Gruyère, finely grated (1½ cups)

½ cup plus 1 Tbsp [135 ml] cold buttermilk

often, until fragrant. Add the onion and a big pinch of salt and cook, stirring frequently, until the onion softens and becomes translucent, 10 to 12 minutes. If the onion begins to brown too quickly, lower the heat to medium-low. Add the white wine and cook until the liquid evaporates, 2 to 3 minutes. If using vinegar, add an additional 1½ Tbsp water.

5 Stir in the heavy cream, bring to a simmer over medium-low heat, and cook, stirring occasionally, until it thickens and is slightly reduced, 4 to 5 minutes. Turn the heat to low and stir in ½ cup (2 oz [55 g]) Gruyère, nutmeg, and cayenne. Once the cheese has melted, stir in the greens to fully coat. Season with salt and more cayenne if desired. Remove the thyme sprigs and remove from the heat. Set aside while you make the biscuits.

6 **To make the biscuits:** In a large bowl, whisk together the flour, baking powder, sugar, salt, baking soda, and cayenne. Toss in the butter cubes to fully coat. Working quickly, use a fork or your fingers to cut the butter into the flour until it resembles coarse meal. Add the Gruyère and mix to combine. Make a well in the middle and pour in all the buttermilk. Use a fork to stir it in until the mixture just comes together and resembles a slightly sticky, shaggy dough (you don't want to overmix, or the biscuits won't turn out tender).

7 Using a dinner spoon, drop 6 equally sized mounds of biscuit batter onto the greens. Transfer to the oven and bake until the biscuits begin to brown, 15 to 20 minutes. Remove from the oven, sprinkle evenly with the remaining ¼ cup Gruyère, and continue to bake until the greens are bubbling and the biscuits are golden brown, another 5 to 10 minutes. Let cool slightly before serving directly from the pan.

ZUCCHINI,

PECORINO, AND FETA

FRITTERS

WITH GARLICKY LEMON YOGURT

I love a good crisped-on-the-outside, tender-on-the-inside vegetable fritter: as a snack, a side, or topped with a fried egg for a satisfying breakfast or lunch. In the summertime, I reach for zucchini and add flavors that remind me of my Russian mother's cooking—dill, green onions, garlic, and briny feta—and add bright lemon and sharp pecorino romano to really make these shredded pancakes stand out. I promise that you won't be able to stop at one, especially with a dollop of cooling yogurt sauce. Fortunately, this recipe can easily be doubled and made ahead for the week.

*Makes about ten 2½ to 3 in
[6 to 7.5 cm] fritters*

1 **To make the yogurt sauce:** In a small bowl, stir together the yogurt, garlic, and lemon juice. Season with salt and set aside. The sauce can be stored in an airtight container and refrigerated for 3 or 4 days in advance.

2 In a large bowl, toss the zucchini with 1 tsp of salt and let sit for 15 to 20 minutes.

3 Meanwhile, preheat the oven to 250°F [120°C]. Set a wire rack in a large rimmed baking sheet or line a rimmed baking sheet with parchment paper. Line a plate with paper towels.

4 When the zucchini is ready, squeeze handfuls of the squash over the sink to remove as much liquid as possible (the more liquid removed, the crispier these will be!). Season with salt, if needed, and Aleppo pepper. Stir in the green onions, garlic, dill, lemon zest, pecorino, feta, and egg. In a separate small bowl, whisk together the flour and baking powder. Stir the flour mixture into the zucchini mixture and toss until just combined.

-cont.

GARLICKY LEMON YOGURT

1 cup [260 g] whole milk Greek yogurt

1 garlic clove, minced or finely grated

1 Tbsp fresh lemon juice

Kosher salt

—

1 lb [455 g] zucchini or any summer squash, ends trimmed, shredded (about 2 medium zucchini)

Kosher salt

Aleppo pepper or red pepper flakes, plus more for garnish

2 green onions, cut into thin slices

1 garlic clove, minced

1½ Tbsp finely chopped fresh dill, or 2 Tbsp finely chopped basil

1½ tsp lemon zest

1 oz [30 g] pecorino romano cheese, medium grated (about ⅓ cup)

1½ oz [40 g] crumbled feta (about ⅓ cup)

1 large egg, lightly beaten

½ cup [70 g] all-purpose or gluten-free flour

½ tsp baking powder

¼ cup [60 ml] canola or grapeseed oil, plus more as needed

5 In a large cast-iron skillet or frying pan, heat the oil over medium heat until shimmering. Working in batches of 3 or 4, take large spoonfuls of the zucchini mixture and drop them into the hot oil—don't overcrowd the pan. Carefully flatten each dollop with the back of your spoon to create a flat disk. Cook until the bottom is crispy and golden, 2 to 3 minutes. Flip and fry them on the other side until browned, another 2 to 3 minutes.

6 Transfer briefly to the paper towel–lined plate to drain before moving them to the prepared baking sheet. Keep in the warm oven until ready to serve. Repeat the process, adding more oil to the pan as needed.

7 Serve immediately, warm or at room temperature, with the yogurt sauce and Aleppo pepper for sprinkling. Stored in an airtight container, the cooked fritters can be refrigerated for up to 1 week or frozen for up to 3 months. When ready to eat, simply spread them out on a baking sheet and heat them in a 350°F [180°C] oven until they're hot and crisp again.

RICE CASSEROLE

This comforting rice casserole dish is one part hot cheesy goodness, one part nostalgia, and 100 percent easy and quick to put together. The original recipe comes from Margaret Anne Eschenroeder, my partner's mother, but I couldn't help but put my own twist on it with the addition of bright cilantro and the swapping of Parmesan for Cotija—its salty, aged Mexican counterpart.

Serves 4

1 Preheat the oven to 350°F [180°C]. Butter an 8 by 11 in [17 by 28 cm] casserole dish.

2 Cook the rice according to package directions or in a rice cooker. The rice can be made up to 4 days in advance.

3 Mix the rice with the sour cream, chiles, and cilantro in a large bowl. Season with salt and black pepper. Evenly spread half of the mixture in the prepared casserole dish. Top with an even layer of the Monterey Jack and cover with the remaining rice mixture. Top with an even layer of the Cotija and sprinkle with paprika.

4 Cover tightly with foil and bake for 30 minutes. Remove the foil and serve immediately.

1 cup [200 g] jasmine rice, rinsed well and drained

1 cup [240 g] sour cream

Two 4 oz [115 g] cans diced Hatch green chiles

½ cup [10 g] roughly chopped fresh cilantro leaves

Kosher salt

Freshly ground black pepper

4 to 6 oz [115 to 170 g] Monterey Jack cheese, coarsely grated (1 to 1½ cups)

2 oz [55 g] crumbled Cotija cheese (a little less than ½ cup) or coarsely grated fresh Parmesan cheese (about ½ cup)

Paprika, regular or smoked

CHEDDAR, SOUR CREAM, AND ONION HASSELBACK

POTATO GRATIN

The way the potatoes are thinly sliced and stacked together in this visually impressive gratin reminds me of chips—which is why I was inspired to flavor them as if they were. You might raise your eyebrow and think that this dish is too complicated, but in reality, a mandoline makes quick work of assembly—it's the long bake you'll have to allot time for. Thankfully, it's worth it. The potatoes turn out creamy and tender on the bottom and crispy, browned, and cheesy on top. It's comfort food at its best and will quickly earn its keep on any holiday table.

Depending on the shape of your pan and potatoes, the amount of potatoes you'll need to fit your dish will vary. I recommend buying an extra potato or two in case they're necessary. Original method comes from J. Kenji López-Alt.

Serves 4

1 Preheat the oven to 400°F [200°C] and generously butter or oil a 7 by 11 in [17 by 28 cm] rectangular or oval casserole dish.

2 In a large bowl, mix together the heavy cream, sour cream, all but 1 Tbsp of the chives, the onion, garlic, salt (it may seem like a lot, but it's not!), and onion powder until combined. Season generously with black pepper. The mixture will taste like an intensely seasoned sour cream and onion chip. Stir in two-thirds of both the Cheddar and the Parmesan cheeses.

3 Add all the potato slices and gently toss until they are evenly coated. If any slices are stuck together, make sure to separate to coat them.

4 Take a handful of potato slices, organize them into a neat stack, and place them in the casserole dish with the edges vertically aligned. Continue this process, working around the perimeter and then filling the

-cont.

1 cup [240 ml] heavy cream

1 cup [240 g] sour cream

1 bunch chives, minced (about ¼ cup [15 g])

½ small yellow or red onion, finely chopped

2 garlic cloves, minced

1 Tbsp kosher salt

2 tsp onion powder

Freshly ground black pepper

6 oz [170 g]) sharp Cheddar cheese, coarsely grated (1½ cups)

2 oz [55 g] fresh Parmesan cheeese, coarsely grated (about ½ cup)

4½ to 5 lb [2 to 2.3 kg] russet potatoes (5 or 6 large), peeled and cut into ⅛ in [4 mm] slices

center, until all the slices are used and tightly packed. If you need more potato, peel and slice another one, coat the slices in the sour cream mixture, and add them to the dish.

5 Once you're done filling the pan, you'll find that the sour cream mixture will pool at the bottom. You want it to reach about halfway up the sides of dish—if it doesn't, pour the remaining mixture into the pan until it reaches that mark. If it fills more than halfway, try spooning out as much as possible. Any more liquid than that, and it'll bubble over in the oven, burn, and fill your house with smoke.

6 Tightly cover the dish in foil and bake for 30 minutes. Remove the foil and bake for another 30 to 35 minutes, until the potatoes are lightly golden. Remove from the oven, sprinkle with the remaining cheese, and bake until deeply golden and crisp, another 30 minutes. Let sit for 5 to 10 minutes before garnishing with the reserved chives and serving.

EGG-PLANT

INVOLTINI WITH PESTO, RICOTTA, AND MOZZARELLA

This eggplant involtini, the Italian word for anything wrapped into small bundles, is as weeknight-friendly as they come. No frying means less mess and a lighter dish, and pesto in the creamy ricotta and mozzarella filling packs a punch of flavor without any of the effort of chopping or zesting extra ingredients. Stuff the eggplant slices, nestle them into your favorite store-bought tomato sauce, bake, and finish with a blanket of fresh mozzarella. Now that's *amore!*

Serves 4 to 6

1 Position racks in the upper and bottom thirds of the oven and preheat to 375°F [190°C].

2 Sprinkle both sides of the eggplant slices with salt. Let sit on a large plate for 15 minutes before patting completely dry with a paper towel. Divide the slices between two large baking sheets and arrange in an even layer. Generously brush both sides of each slice with olive oil and bake until fork tender, 25 to 30 minutes, flipping the eggplant and swapping and rotating the sheets halfway through. Remove from the oven and let cool.

3 Meanwhile, in a medium bowl, mix the ricotta, pesto, low-moisture mozzarella, and egg until combined. Season with pepper (I usually find it doesn't need salt). Set aside.

4 Spoon 1 cup [240 ml] of the tomato sauce in an even layer in a 9 by 13 in [23 by 33 cm] baking dish (or another shallow dish that will snuggly fit the eggplant rolls).

5 Spoon a heaping 1 Tbsp of the ricotta mixture at the widest end of an eggplant slice. Roll up and place, seam-side down, in the baking dish. Repeat until all the eggplant slices are rolled up. Top with the remaining 2 cups [480 ml] tomato sauce.

6 Bake for 20 to 25 minutes. Remove from the oven, top with an even layer of the fresh mozzarella, and return to the oven to bake for another 10 minutes, or until the eggplant is bubbling and the cheese has melted. Allow to sit for 5 to 10 minutes before serving.

---

3 medium eggplant (about 3 lb [1.4 kg]), trimmed and cut lengthwise into ½ in [12 mm] slices (about 18 slices total)

Kosher salt

Extra-virgin olive oil

1 cup [240 g] whole milk ricotta

¼ cup [65 g] pesto

4 oz [115 g] low-moisture whole milk mozzarella, coarsely grated (1 cup)

1 egg, lightly beaten

Freshly ground black pepper

One 24 oz [720 ml] jar store-bought marinara sauce

One 8 oz [230 g] ball fresh mozzarella, cut into thin slices

ACKNOWLEDGMENTS

As with anything that I do, I couldn't have written this book without the support and encouragement of my family and friends. A big thanks to:

My mom, for showing me not only that with hard work and resourcefulness I can achieve anything I set my sights on, but also what it means to be resilient and keep going no matter what life throws at me.

My wonderful friends and community—in Rhode Island, Boston, Charlottesville, New York, Seattle, the list goes on—for believing in me, even when I myself didn't. Special shout-out to Kelsey for always being game to be my sounding board, unofficial editor, and shoulder to cry on.

The ladies of *Culture Magazine*—Lassa, Stephanie, Becca, and especially Molly—for seeing my potential and taking me on as an intern that fateful fall and unknowingly setting me down the path that brought me here, many wheels and wedges later. I wouldn't be an official curd nerd without you all! Also, Sara Adduci, for igniting that initial spark and for fostering my love and curiosity for (and let's face it, addiction to) cheese through all these years.

My editors, Deanne Katz and Dena Rayess, for taking a chance on me and helping me fulfill a lifelong dream of writing a cookbook. And I can't forget the talented team of photographers, stylists, and designers for bringing this book to life.

My recipes wouldn't be as foolproof or nearly as strong without my recipe testers: Sara, Mom, Kelsey, Naz, Jen, Naomi, Chelsea, Ana, Anuja, Ayako, Della, Molly, Anne, Kristen and Peter, Anna, Chelsey, Janey, PK, Leigh, Elise, Juan and Casey, Laura, and Colleen. Your feedback is what kept me going. I want to especially thank Kate Malay for being relentless in her willingness to test for me, for being meticulous in her work, and for never being afraid to critique and push me to do better. You're the best, girl!

Last but not least, thank you, Lee, and your lightning-speed metabolism and stomach of steel. I can't think of a single person who could've kept up with the amount of hot cheese I was producing while testing. Whether it was eleven thirty at night or eight in the morning after a twenty-eight-hour shift at the hospital, you always met whatever bite I forced on you with gratitude and enthusiasm. Thank you for being my voice of reason, rock, and No. 1 recipe taster—your patience and steadfastness through this roller coaster deserves all the gold stars in the world.

AUTHOR BIO

Polina Chesnakova is a Seattle-based food writer, recipe developer, and cooking class instructor whose work has been featured in *Culture*, the *Washington Post*, *Saveur*, *Kitchn*, and *Seattle* magazine.

FAVORITE WAY TO EAT HOT CHEESE:

Nachos!

FAVORITE GUILTY CHEESE PLEASURE:

Raclette

FAVORITE CHEESE:

Gruyère (melted) and Halloumi

FAVORITE HOT CHEESE DISH TO SHARE:

Chorizo, Sweet Potato, and Kale Enchiladas

INDEX